MATHS GAMES

KEY STAGE ONE 1

Number

Joe Santaniello

Published by Scholastic Publications Ltd,
Villiers House, Clarendon Avenue,
Leamington Spa, Warwickshire CV32 5PR
© 1995 Scholastic Publications Ltd

AUTHOR Joe Santaniello
EDITOR Noel Pritchard
ASSISTANT EDITORS Joel Lane and Joanne Boden
SERIES DESIGNER Joy White
DESIGNERS Toby Long and Tracey Ramsey
ILLUSTRATIONS Lorna Kent
COVER ARTWORK Joy White

Designed using Aldus Pagemaker
Processed by Pages Bureau, Leamington Spa
Printed in Great Britain by Bell & Bain Ltd, Glasgow

British Library Cataloguing-in-Publication Data
A catalogue record for this book is available from the British Library.

ISBN 0-590-53358-4

Contents

Contents...

MATHS GAMES
KEY STAGE ONE
1
GAMES

Introduction

THE CONTRIBUTION OF GAMES TO TEACHING AND LEARNING

We live in a games-saturated culture. Outdoor sports and computer games are obvious examples at opposite ends of a spectrum that encompasses our everyday life. Games appeal to all sections of society, and are therefore levellers of difference. But games are often ephemeral. We play them. We forget them. Perhaps it is this transience which makes some teachers and parents sceptical of the value games have in learning. Games in school are often relegated to a peripheral role, as time-fillers or rewards for having completed 'important' work. The books in this series are an attempt to counterbalance this viewpoint by showing how games with clear learning objectives can be brought into the mainstream of primary teaching, to help develop key concepts and skills alongside any scheme of work.

In the context of mathematics teaching, games serve a number of educational purposes, providing an alternative forum for:
- using and applying mathematical skills and understanding;
- discussing mathematical concepts and developing mathematical language;
- developing the ability to follow instructions;
- developing co-operative learning, social and problem-solving skills;
- increasing motivation and subject interest;
- encouraging independence;
- bridging the gap between practical activities and more abstract methods of recording;
- assessing acquisition of skills and knowledge.

The games in this series of books also offer the following benefits. They:
- have clear educational objectives linked to the National Curriculum programmes of study and the Scottish 5-14 Guidelines;
- save time and money by providing photocopiable resources;
- can be adapted to suit individual needs and purposes;
- offer suggestions for differentiation;
- include game record sheets to promote data handling and record-keeping, and to provide evidence;
- have lively real-life and imaginary contexts to capture and hold the children's interest.

GAMES AND THE MATHEMATICS CURRICULUM

All of these games have been devised to support Mathematics requirements in the National Curriculum and the Scottish 5-14 Guidelines. A vital element of many traditional games is the reinforcement of counting and number recognition skills. The games in this series build on these acknowledged benefits, extending them into less well-explored areas of the Mathematics curriculum within an atmosphere of pleasurable learning. The children's imagination is captured by interlacing the mathematical content with role-playing in both 'real' and fantasy worlds. The games provide a collaborative forum for discussion and, therefore, a focus for asking questions and developing mathematical language. The decision-making, prediction and reasoning skills outlined in Using and Applying Mathematics (Attainment Target 1) are developed in all the games, and the inclusion of game record sheets ensures that data handling is integrated throughout.

THE GAMES

This book contains both non-board based games (in the section called 'Activity games') as well as games that use boards and other manipulative resources (in the sections called 'Photocopiable games' and 'Special section').

ACTIVITY GAMES

This section provides a selection of ideas for games that only require resources commonly found in classrooms. Most of the games can be played by the whole class. Some are physical activity games and are best played in a large open space such as a hall, playground or field.

PHOTOCOPIABLE GAMES

The games in this section are based on photocopiable resources that are provided. These resources include game boards (some of which have a three-dimensional element), cards, game rules, game record sheets, and playing components such as spinners and playing pieces. These games follow traditional game formats and are designed to be played in small groups. The 'make-your-own' feature of the photocopiable sheets means that games can be adapted easily and without great expense.

When making the playing pieces, cut along solid lines and fold along dotted lines.

The following symbols are used on some of the photocopiable pages:

 A calculator may be useful.

 For construction, the sheet needs to be photocopied the number of times shown.

SPECIAL SECTION

This section contains photocopiable resources to be used with games from the 'Photocopiable games' section. They also have wider applications for other mathematics and cross-curricular activities.

THE TEACHERS' NOTES

The teachers' notes follow a standard format for each game:

TEACHING CONTENT

The mathematical learning objectives are signposted and linked to the National Curriculum programmes of study for Key Stage One and the Scottish 5-14 Guidelines. For example: **(N: 3c; AS: B)** indicates National Curriculum Attainment Target **N**umber: Key Stage One programme of study paragraph **3c**; Scottish 5-14 Guidelines for Number, Money and Measurement, strand **A**ddition and **S**ubtraction, Level **B**.

WHAT YOU NEED

Resources that you will need are listed under the following headings: 'Photocopiable sheets', 'For construction' and 'For playing'. It is recommended that where coins are needed, these be plastic or card play models.

PREPARATION

Notes are given on assembling the game and, where appropriate, suggestions made for introducing the game.

HOW TO PLAY

The aim and rules of the game are briefly summarised and any additional information for the teacher to consider is pointed out.

TEACHER'S ROLE

In some of the games the teacher is an active participant, in others a facilitator or an observer. This section helps the teacher to define her role and offers ideas for developing the game's mathematical ideas and skills. See also page 9.

GAME VARIATIONS

Where a game can be varied within the mathematical objectives set out under the 'Teaching content', ideas are given.

EXTENSION

Where a game might be extended to develop the mathematical objectives, ideas are given.

ASSESSMENT

There are three main ways that the teacher can assess the value of a game and the children's learning:

• Direct observation of the game in progress
Observation of a game allows the teacher to note how each child copes with the skills required in the game. A clipboard is handy for on-the-spot jotting down of notes. Be aware, however, that an adult presence can distort the game.

• Discussion after the game
After the game, the supervising adult can discuss what happened with

the group, extending the players' horizons beyond the 'who won' mentality. Where appropriate, pointers and suggested questions for doing this are given in the teachers' notes.

• Using game record sheets

Many games are accompanied by a game record sheet upon which the result and how it was achieved can be recorded by the players themselves, giving concrete evidence of how well they have assimilated the concept(s) behind the game. The game record sheets employ writing, drawing and data handling skills to give the busy teacher an outline of the completed game; in many cases, these sheets can be adapted to provide differentiation for the games.

CLASSROOM MANAGEMENT

As indicated above, not all the games are board games. There are card games, pencil and paper games, calculator games and mental games. This variety enables the teacher to select the appropriate game for the particular classroom situation, or even for sending home to be played with parents. Group games can be played at a table or in a designated corner. Some games are suitable for individual play – a copy of a single track, for instance, can be used both as a playing surface and as a record of the game – with the child competing against herself.

THE TEACHER'S ROLE

The teacher's main task will be in the selection of the game and the setting up of play for the designated educational purpose. She will need to decide what curricular function the game can serve. It can introduce a subject; it can reinforce skills or knowledge already touched on; or it can be a means of assessment. Most of the games and all the game record sheets are ideal for assessment; suggestions for carrying this out are given, where appropriate, within the teachers' notes for each game.

Unless the children have played the game before, or are competent readers and can play well together on their own, the teacher (or another adult) will need to introduce and supervise the games. Ideas for introducing the games are given, where appropriate, in the teachers' notes to provide a context or stimulus for playing the game. Alternatively, the teacher can make up her own.

There is no sense in letting children play a game and then forget it. It needs to be followed up. In the teachers' notes for each game, there are suggestions about the part the supervising adult can play in enlarging the players' horizons beyond the actual playing of the game.

Obviously, the light of experience will indicate possible variations to the games, and the photocopiable pages enable the teacher to alter details and change rules to match individual needs and purposes.

MAKING AND STORING THE GAMES

Photocopiable games are flexible and inexpensive. Even elaborate board games can be made for pence, whereas comparable commercial games would cost pounds. Also, little more than the usual art materials found in most schools is needed for their construction. So instead of having just a few games to enhance motivation and learning, the teacher can afford to be quite lavish with them.

If possible, photocopy the game boards and playing pieces directly on to card.

The appearance and motivational benefit of the games can be greatly improved by colouring them in. Felt-tipped pens are best as they don't warp the paper as much as paint. Laminating the game boards and pieces also improves appearance and increases durability.

• Using parents and educational assistants

There is no reason why the teacher needs to do all the assembling. Games construction is a pleasurable activity involving colouring-in, cutting, pasting and, optionally, laminating. None of these tasks requires a teaching certificate! Parents, and even older pupils in the school, are quite capable of doing most of these things. Organise a games-making event involving both parents and pupils!

Similarly, a parent can be the games supervisor, instructing the group in the rules of the game, keeping an eye on its progress and conducting the discussion afterwards.

• Storing the games

Keep the various components of each game (board, pieces, game record sheets, 'How to play' sheets, and so on) in an individual strong polythene bag, fastened with a wire tie. These can be attached to a 'Mathematics games' board with a small bulldog clip (as shown in the illustration). Alternatively, the games can be stored in boxes – either kept individually or grouped according to difficulty in a large box and separated using coloured dividers.

ADAPTING THE GAMES

Photocopiable games are easily adapted. They can be changed to suit different purposes and abilities. You need not be stuck with a resource that only meets a small percentage of your requirements. Just delete the bit you don't want by covering with liquid paper or a sticky label, then draw and/or print your modification on top. If you are altering very fine detail, enlarge the sheet before making the alterations. Do your alterations on the enlargement, making sure to draw the lines the same density and thickness as the enlargement. Then reduce back to original size. Similarly, if a game is too big or too small, it can be altered to size using the enlarging or reducing facility on large photocopiers. If yours won't do this, ones that will can be found in most public libraries.

Simple alterations such as writing children's names on playing pieces or using the school logo on the headings may seem small things in themselves, but they make the games more personal and special.

Copies of each adaptation can be kept in polypockets in an A4 ring binder devoted to the purpose. A slip of paper or card can be put in the pocket detailing when the adaptation was made, its curriculum focus, which class used it, notes on how effective it was and further ideas for adaptation.

CROSS-CURRICULAR CONNECTIONS

As many of the games involve role-playing and have suitable contexts to develop storylines, they fit easily into language topics. Some of the games will readily integrate with other subject areas – for example, 'It's a frog's life' with science and 'Round the block' with geography.

LINKS TO THE NATIONAL CURRICULUM

● main game
○ extension

Games	Programme of Study																		
	1a	1b	1c	1d	1e	2a	2b	2c	3a	3b	3c	3d	3e	4a	4b	4c	4d	5a	5b
Counting rhymes	●					●	●			●	●	●							
Birth dates	●					●	●											●	
Swap it			●		●	●													
'The' game	●						●												
Coin bank														●					
Mental maths											●	●							
Add it up											●	●							●
Claim a number										●	●								
Multiples stand up						●				●									
Coin flowers			●														●	●	
Colour caterpillar				○		●			●			○	○					○	○
Bag of ten						●	●												
Clothes line									●										
Bus stop						●				●		●							
Identikit						●				●	●			●					
Fire! Fire!	●					○	●			●									○
Hop it!	●					●		○	●	●									
To buy a fat pig	●					●					●	●		●					
To market, to market				○	●	●		○			●	●	○	●	○				●
Bingo 100					●		●												
Bull's eye						●	●			●				●					
Fair's fare														●					
Soldiers on parade	●					●	●			●	●						○		
Penny purse	●		●			●	●		●	●	○			○	●				
Pound purse	●					●				●				●	●				
Odds & evens hoopla				●		●													
Gone fishing	●									●									
High or low?			●									●				●			
Round the block											●		●			●	●		
It's a frog's life						●	●					●							
Piece of cake								●											
Multiplication bingo											●		●						
Space rangers	●									●									
Stop and shop	●			●		●		○			●			●	○				●
Storywood stars	●										●			●					

11

LINKS TO SCOTTISH 5–14 GUIDELINES

● main game
○ extension

Games	Attainment target and outcomes												
	RTN A	RTN B	RTN C	PS A	PS B	AS A	AS B	AS C	M A	M B	MD B	MD C	FE B
Counting rhymes	●			●		●							
Birth dates	●	●				●							
Swap it	●												
'The' game	●	●				●							
Coin bank							●			●			
Mental maths							●						
Add it up						●	●						
Claim a number					●						●		
Multiples stand up											●		
Coin flowers										●			
Colour caterpillar				●			○						
Bag of ten	●			●									
Clothes line				●									
Bus stop	●					●							
Identikit	●					●	●						
Fire! Fire!	●	●		○	○	●	●						
Hop it!	●	●				●	●						
To buy a fat pig	●						●						
To market, to market	●	○	○				●			○			
Bingo 100		●											
Bull's eye	●						●						
Fair's fare									●	●			
Soldiers on parade				●		●	●						
Penny purse	●	○				●	○		●	●	○		
Pound purse		●					●		●	●			
Odds & evens hoopla	●				●								
Gone fishing	●						●						
High or low?							●	●					
Round the block							●				●		
It's a frog's life	●	●					●						
Piece of cake		●											
Multiplication bingo											●	●	
Space rangers					●								●
Stop and shop	●		○			●	●			●		○	
Storywood stars						●							●

MATHS GAMES

KEY STAGE ONE

Activity games

COUNTING RHYMES

TEACHING CONTENT

The natural appeal of rhymes and the opportunities they provide for active involvement make them ideal as a means of teaching across the curriculum. Counting rhymes are particularly useful in maths for:

☆ Introducing mathematical language (UA: 1a)
☆ Developing familiarity with number names (N: 1a; RTN: A)
☆ Counting orally (N: 2a; RTN: A)
☆ Ordering number (N: 2b; RTN: A)
☆ Exploring patterns and recognising sequences (N: 1a, 2a; PS: A)
☆ Introducing knowledge and use of simple addition and subtraction facts (N: 3b, c, d; AS: A)

Each of the following activity games is based on a counting rhyme, and is thematically linked to one of the games in the 'Photocopiable games' section so that, if desired, it can be used as an introductory activity. The game to which it is linked is given in brackets after the title. Most of these counting rhyme games are whole-class activities and require a large playing space, either in the classroom or in a hall.

TEACHING THE RHYMES

Share the rhymes with the children. These can be taught at any time as a whole-class activity. Recite aloud the rhyme you wish to teach and ask the children to listen carefully. Then repeat it bit by bit with the children reciting after you. Discuss any unfamiliar vocabulary with the children, for example 'sow' in the first rhyme.

---

1. THERE ONCE WAS A SOW (TO BUY A FAT PIG)

There was once a sow
Who had one little pig,
And one little pig had she.
And that old sow went 'Umph',
And the little pig went 'Wee'!

There was once a sow
Who had two little pigs,
And two little pigs had she.
And that old sow went 'Umph',
And the little pigs went 'Wee, Wee'!

And so on, to ten little pigs saying 'Wee, Wee, Wee, Wee, Wee, Wee, Wee, Wee, Wee, Wee'!

WHAT YOU NEED

No special equipment required.

HOW TO PLAY

Choose two children to play the parts of the sow and the first little pig. The whole group recites the first verse, and at the end the first little pig chooses a second little pig from the group. They all chant the second verse and, at the end, the second little pig chooses a third little pig, and so on until there are 10 little pigs. Initially, each of the 'characters' can say their own 'umph' and 'wee'. This not only reinforces one-to-one correspondence, but also makes it easier for those who have difficulty keeping track of the number of 'wees' needed! (You could also, of course, reduce the total number of pigs, so that the rhyme finishes after, say, five.) However, it heightens the fun and excitement if they can work towards unison recitation – and get the number of 'wees' right each time!

TEACHER'S ROLE

The rhyme adds one to each number in progression from 1 to 10, and the children have to make a one-to-one correspondence between the number of pigs and the number of wees. Ask them, for example: When the sow has four little pigs, how many 'wees' must you say? If there are more than eleven children in the group (i.e. sow + 10 pigs), ask the children if they can *all* be piglets. Why not?

Make a number sentence on the board or with large cards to show how an 'adding story' builds up: 1 + 1 + 1 and so on. Use appropriate mathematical vocabulary such as 'add' (rather than 'and') and 'equals' (rather than 'makes').

2. TEN TALL SOLDIERS (SOLDIERS ON PARADE)

Ten tall soldiers
Standing in a row.
Nine stood up
And one lay low.
Along came the sergeant
And what do you think?
Up popped the other one
Quick as a wink.

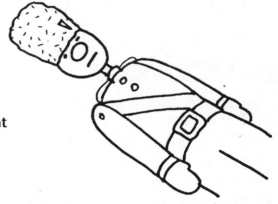

Ten tall soldiers
Standing in a row.
Eight stood up
And two lay low.
Along came the sergeant
And what do you think?
Up popped the other ones
Quick as a wink.

And so on, until...

Ten tall soldiers
Standing in a row.
None stood up
And ten lay low.
Along came the sergeant
And what do you think?
Up they all popped
Quick as a wink.

HOW TO PLAY

Ten children are chosen to play the parts of the soldiers and an eleventh (or the teacher) to play the part of the sergeant. Ask the children if they know how soldiers stand to attention and walk, and encourage them to act out the rhyme in their roles as the rest of the class recite it. As a variation, and to highlight the number bonds illustrated, divide the part of the class that is reciting into two groups. Both groups recite the rhyme together, except for lines 3 and 4 of each verse. One group says line 3 and the other says line 4.

TEACHER'S ROLE

This is an excellent game for exploring and learning the number bonds for ten and for providing a visual demonstration of the concept that subtraction is the inverse of addition. Initially, if they are able, allow the children to recite and act the rhyme all the way through, noting any problems they have in determining how many stand up and how many lay low. Ask the children: What is happening in each verse? Try to elicit from them the pattern that emerges: reducing the number of standing soldiers by 1, while increasing the number of soldiers laying low by 1, each time. How many soldiers are standing at the end of each verse? Repeat the rhyme, stopping at the end of each verse to talk about the related number bonds for ten. Write the subtraction number sentence for each one, and see if the children can say what the addition sentence would be when the 'laying low' soldiers pop up at the end.

3. TEN CURRANT BUNS (PENNY PURSE)

Ten currant buns in the baker's shop,
Round and fat with sugar on the top.
Along came [name of child] with a penny one day,
Bought a currant bun and took it away.

Nine currant buns in the baker's shop,
Round and fat with sugar on the top.
Along came [name of child] with a penny one day,
Bought a currant bun and took it away.

And so on, until...

No currant buns in the baker's shop,
Round and fat with sugar on the top.
No one came along with a penny to pay,
So the baker went home for the rest of the day.

WHAT YOU NEED

A table, ten 1p coins, till, ten currant buns (real or card), a baker's hat and props for customers (optional).

HOW TO PLAY

Ten children are chosen to play the parts of the customers, and one to be the baker. Add to the fun of the role play by giving the baker a baker's hat, a tray of currant buns (real or card) and a 'till', and the customers various bits of costume or props and a 1p coin each.

The ten customers queue up to one side of the 'shop'. One by one, as the rest of the class recites the rhyme, the customers give their money to the baker and she gives them a bun. The customers then form a queue on the other side of the shop. At the end of the game, ask: How much money has the baker got? Count out the coins from the baker's till.

TEACHER'S ROLE

Not only is this game a simple example of subtraction as the inverse of addition, but it also provides a role play experience that develops the concept of exchange – in this case, money being exchanged for goods. Initially, let the children play through the whole rhyme. Then repeat the activity, stopping at strategic points to ask: How many children have bought buns? Therefore, how many pennies does the baker have? How much money is this? How many buns are still left to buy? At the end of the rhyme, how much money will the baker have? Let's count the money to see.

When the class becomes familiar with the game, adapt it by, for instance, varying the number of customers and/or the amount of money each has to spend. Adapt the rhyme accordingly. This will lead the class to explore the different number bonds of ten.

4. HERE COMES THE BUS (BUS STOP)

Here comes the bus,
It's going to stop.
Hurry up, children,
In you pop.
Five in the queue, none inside,
Any more now, before we ride?

Here is the bus,
It has to stop.
Hurry up, children,
In you pop.
Four in the queue, one inside,
Any more now, before we ride?

And so on, until...

Here is the bus,
It has to stop.
Hurry up, children,
In you pop.
None in the queue and five inside,
No more now, away we ride!

WHAT YOU NEED
Bus driver's hat and props for passengers.

HOW TO PLAY

The numbers given for the rhyme fit the photocopiable game 'Bus stop', but could be adapted for your own purposes. For the purposes of the game as given, six children are chosen: one to play the bus driver/bus and five to play the passengers. The line of passengers waits patiently for the 'bus' to arrive. As the class recites the first verse, the bus draws up to the queue. During the second verse, on 'In you pop', the first passenger in the queue gets behind the bus driver and holds on to his waist. The 'bus' and passenger move off around the room. The third verse is then recited; on 'In you pop', the second passenger joins on, holding on to the waist of the first passenger. When the five passengers have all 'boarded' their bus, the whole busload snakes off around the room.

If there are enough children in the class, divide them into equal-sized groups and let the whole class perform the role play.

TEACHER'S ROLE

This game is easily adapted for exploring and learning various number bonds and for providing a visual demonstration of the concept that subtraction is the inverse of addition. Initially, if they are able, allow the children to recite and act the rhyme all the way through, noting any problems they have in determining who boards next. Ask the children: What is happening in each verse? Try to elicit from them the pattern that emerges: reducing the number of people in the queue by 1, while increasing the number of passengers on the bus by 1. How many people are still in the queue at the end of each verse? Repeat the rhyme, stopping at the end of each verse to talk about the related number bonds. Write the subtraction number sentence for each verse and see if the children can say what the related addition sentence would be.

BIRTH DATES

TEACHING CONTENT

☆ Developing flexible methods of working with number, orally and mentally (N: 1a; AS: A)
☆ Counting collections of objects (N: 2a; RTN: A, B)
☆ Reading and ordering numbers to 100 (N: 2b; RTN: A, B)
☆ Sorting (N: 5a; IH: A)

PREPARATION

This is a class game that is best played in a hall or other large space. Provide each child with a label with a loop of string fastened to each end so it can be hung round the neck. For each child, print her birth date in three different colours in the sequence: day number (red)/month number (blue)/year number (green) – for example, 27/9/89. (Some children may be able to make their own.) Explain what this convention for writing dates means, and make sure they understand the numbers representing the months.

WHAT YOU NEED

Enough card labels (approx. 15cm x 11cm) for each child, string, adhesive tape, red, blue and green coloured pencils or crayons.

HOW TO PLAY

Divide the children into two teams. Tell them that the game consists of several activities. Points will be awarded for each activity correctly done, and the team with the most points at the end wins.

1. Children look at the middle (blue) numbers on their labels and sort themselves into groups of like number – for example, all those with a blue 2 together, all those with a blue 11 together, and so on. Explain that some 'groups' may only consist of one person if that is the only person on that team born in that month. When they have done this, they should sit down. The first team to sit down wins a point, *provided* they have grouped themselves correctly.

2. Children stay in their previously-formed groups (by month), but now they have to order the groups from lowest to highest. Explain that there may be some numbers missing – for example, if no one was born in May there will be no number 5 group. Instead of sitting down when they've finished, they should raise their hands.

3. Now children look at their red numbers (the day of birth) and sort themselves into the following groups: 1–9, 10–19, 20–29, 30–31. Discuss with them why you have not gone beyond 31. When they have done this, they should sit down.

4. Children stay in their last groups (day of birth), but now they have to put themselves in number order, from lowest to highest. Explain that there may be some numbers missing, or more than one of a number. Instead of sitting down when they've finished, they should raise their hands.

5. Children now look at the green number (year of birth) and sort themselves into groups of like numbers.

TEACHER'S ROLE

Throughout the game, ask the children relevant questions which require them to examine the real context of this sorting and ordering game. For example: How many months are there in a year? Therefore, what will be the highest possible blue number? Do all months have the same number of days? What is the highest number of days in a month? Are there any number gaps in their ordering and sorting? Why is this? What are the missing numbers? What is the highest/lowest number the children have? Why are the groups so large for the year of birth activity?

GAME VARIATION

The game could be extended to practise addition by giving children a target number and asking them to group themselves to make this number, using either the day of birth or the month of birth numbers.

FOLLOW-UP

Make a class birthday graph on which every child's birth date is represented.

SWAP IT

TEACHING CONTENT

☆ Using practical resources to count collections and check totals (N: 1c, 2a; RTN: A)
☆ Developing an understanding that the position of a digit signifies its value (N: 2b; RTN: A)
☆ Introducing counting in tens (N: 2a; RTN: A)

WHAT YOU NEED

A 1 to 6 dice, two sheets of paper, a pencil, collections of three different small items – for example, buttons, paper-clips, small coloured bricks.

PREPARATION

This is a game for two or more players. For each player, you will need to provide a 'place value grid' that is headed with the chosen collectable items (as shown in the example below).

HOW TO PLAY

The players take it in turns to throw the dice, then collect from the pool that number of objects representing the 'ones' column (buttons in the example below) and put them in the correct section on their grid. When they have ten buttons they can swap them for a paper-clip, putting the ten buttons back into the pool. When they have ten paper-clips they can swap them for a small coloured brick. The first player to collect three coloured bricks is the winner.

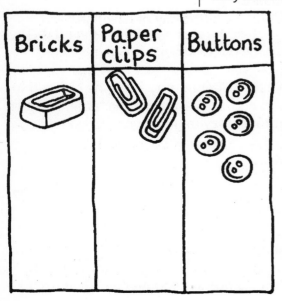

TEACHER'S ROLE

Explain the rules to the children before they begin, making sure they understand the concept of exchange involved. During the game, listen to the children's conversation, noting whether they calculate in advance what number they need to make the next set of ten, or whether they are still at the stage of counting on in ones after the dice has been thrown and before they make their collection. Ask questions such as: How many more buttons do you need to collect a paper-clip? How many buttons did you collect in order to have two paper-clips on your grid? To ascertain whether children understand that more objects does not necessarily mean greater value, ask:

Who is winning? (One child may have eight buttons and one paper-clip, another two paper-clips and one button.)

GAME VARIATIONS

Use 1p, 10p and £1 coins instead of buttons, paper-clips and bricks. These will provide a real example of the number values underlying the game. At the end of the game, the children can talk about what they would spend their money on.

'THE' GAME

TEACHING CONTENT

☆ Developing flexible methods of work with number, orally and mentally (N: 1a; AS: A)
☆ Counting numbers up to 100/1000 (N: 2b; RTN: A, B)

WHAT YOU NEED

A book, paper and a pencil for each player, a calculator.

HOW TO PLAY

This is a game for two players. Give each child a book that has plenty of text. Give the children a target number, depending on their ability (for example: 50, 100, 1000). Each player chooses a page in her book and then, beginning at the top, starts counting the words. When she meets the word 'the', she stops and writes down the number she has reached. She resumes counting, starting from 1 again, until she reaches the next 'the', writing down the number she has reached. These two numbers are added together to keep a running total; then the game continues with each new number being added to the previous total, until the target number is reached (either exactly or if the total goes beyond the target number). The first player to do this is the winner. If the addition is too difficult for some children, let them use a calculator. In any case, a calculator will be useful for checking totals.

Reverse the game. Start at 50: the first person to reach 0 is the winner.

TEACHER'S ROLE

Set a target number that will challenge the children but will not make the game go on too long. Make sure the children understand the importance of keeping a record of their numbers (and the running total) in order to check at the end. After the game, discuss the game record with the children. What was the first number you got? How many more did you then need to get to make the target number? Ask the children to write down all their stopping numbers. For example, if the target number was 50 and they made this exact total, they might have reached it with:

$$1 + 9 + 11 + 7 + 11 + 8 + 3$$

Ask: Does it matter in which order these numbers are added to reach 50? Do the same with the subtraction. For example:

$$50 - 6 - 8 - 11 - 12 - 8 - 5$$

Does it matter in which order these numbers are subtracted? The children should be able to see that the order in which the numbers are processed matters for subtraction, but not for addition. All of the numbers can be added in any order to make the total; but in order for the subtraction to work, they must start with the total (or target number) and work downwards, subtracting from the new total each time. If numbers are subtracted from each other before being subtracted from the total, then the result will be totally different as well as the process being a very confusing one for the children!

COIN BANK

TEACHING CONTENT

☆ Recognising coins and their monetary value (M: B)
☆ Solving problems with whole numbers including money (N: 4a; AS: B)

PREPARATION

Explain to the children that each number on the dice stands for a coin:

= 1p   = 2p   = 5p   = 10p   = 20p   = 50p

This may be difficult for some children to grasp, because of the natural coincidence of 1 = 1p and 2 = 2p. It may help if you explain it in terms of a code. If you think it will be helpful, copy the equivalency chart above and let the children have it near them to refer to when playing the game.

WHAT YOU NEED

A dice and shaker, a collection of 1 to 50p coins and £1 coins, paper and a pencil (optional), a calculator (optional).

HOW TO PLAY

This small-group game is a bit like Snap with dice. In turn, each player throws the dice. When it comes to rest, the first player to call out its monetary value correctly takes a corresponding coin from the bank. If a call is wrong, that player is 'out' for the next throw. The first player to collect a pound's worth of coins swaps them for a £1 coin and wins. However, if the player's coins go beyond £1 (for instance, if a child with 98p calls out correctly for 5p), then he must go on to the next pound. The appropriate strategy for gaining a pound is to consider the money in hand and what coins are needed to win.

TEACHER'S ROLE

The teacher should observe play and note those children who can cope with the dual tasks of the game: making the correlation between numbers on dice and those on coins, and being able to add coins to 100p. If adding the coins mentally is too difficult for some players, they could use paper and pencil or a calculator.

At the end of the game, discuss the various number sentences making £1. It might be advisable, having first talked about 100 1p coins and 50 2p coins, to limit the number of 1p and 2p coins (say five of each). Can any of the children write the coin sentences in dice number code?

MENTAL MATHS

TEACHING CONTENT

★ Practising mental addition and subtraction with numbers to 20 (N: 3c, d; AS: B).

PREPARATION

Two sets of number cards 1–10 are needed. These should be large enough for children to see them easily when they are held up by the teacher (20cm² for example).

HOW TO PLAY

Divide the group into two teams and ask each team to stand in a row. Place the number cards face down in front of you. Pick up the first two cards; but before showing them to the children, say either 'add' or 'subtract'. Then show them the cards. The first child in each team must try to answer the calculation, and the one that does so (correctly) first earns a point for her team. (If the calculation requires subtraction, tell the children always to subtract the smaller number from the larger one.) Those two children then go to the end of their rows, the used cards are shuffled back into the pack and the game continues with the next two children. When all the children have had a go, the team with the most points wins.

TEACHER'S ROLE

Make sure the teams are generally matched in terms of children's maths ability. Those children who are less sure of their addition and/or subtraction facts can then be observed by the teacher without being unduly singled out. The teacher should also keep score, or appoint one member of each team to keep the score for that team. If there is an odd number of children in the group, the remaining child can act as scorekeeper.

GAME VARIATIONS

This game can obviously be adapted for numbers greater than 20 and for multiplication and division as well, depending on the ability of the children. This will, of course, require the use of number cards 1-100 (photocopiable page 69).

ADD IT UP

TEACHING CONTENT

★ Practising mental addition and subtraction (N: 3c, d; AS: A)
★ Keeping a record of scores (N: 5b; AS: B)

PREPARATION

Cover the 6 on each dice with a picture, so that only the numbers 1–5 are available on each.

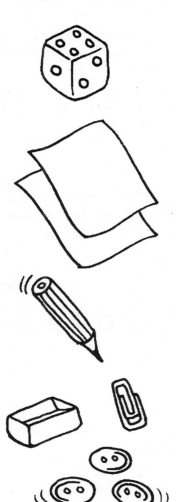

WHAT YOU NEED

Two dice, each with the 6 face covered with a picture; paper and a pencil for each team.

HOW TO PLAY

This is a game for two teams. The children on each team take it in turns to roll the dice. The total number appearing on the two dice becomes the team's score, and each successive roll is added to the previous total. If one of the dice shows the picture face, the most recent addition to the score is subtracted and play passes to the other team. If both picture faces appear, the entire total is lost and play passes to the other team. The first team to reach 100 (or any other predetermined score) wins.

TEACHER'S ROLE

Encourage the children to come to a group decision about what the total of the dice is. Depending on the ability of the children and the predetermined target score, the teacher may need to help with the overall scorekeeping, showing children how to count on from their current scores and encouraging those who can to find other ways of arriving at the total. Encourage the children to talk about how they arrived at their answers, discussing the various methods of mental calculation with them all.

GAME VARIATION

Let each team begin with 100, and subtract the score at each throw from the previous remainder. If one dice shows the picture face, the most recent subtraction is added back on to the total and play passes to the other team. If both picture faces appear, the team's total goes back to 100 and play passes to the other team. The first team to reach 0 wins.

CLAIM A NUMBER

TEACHING CONTENT

★ Practising multiplication facts relating to 2s, 5s and 10s and using these to learn other facts (N: 3c; MD: B)
★ Exploring patterns of multiples (N: 3b; PS: B)

PREPARATION

Use photocopiable page 69 to prepare number cards for a 1 to 100 draw bag. You will also need three large cards, one each with 2×, 5× and 10× written on it.

HOW TO PLAY

Split the class into two or three teams and explain that the object of the game is to claim for their team as many of the numbers you draw from the bag as they can. Explain that before you draw each number, you will show each team one of the three large cards – either the 2×, the 5× or the 10×. They then have to decide whether the number you draw from the bag belongs to that multiplication table. Anyone can claim the number for their team, but it must belong to the multiplication table shown. So, if 15 is drawn out after the 2× card is shown, and someone claims it, that claim is false and the whole team misses the next go. The first team to make a correct claim wins the number. Numbers that no one claims are kept to one side. The first team to get ten numbers wins.

WHAT YOU NEED

Photocopiable sheet 69 (1 to 100 tiles), a bag, three large cards (one each with 2×, 5× and 10× written on it), 3× and 4× cards (optional).

TEACHER'S ROLE

As well as drawing the numbers from the bag, you will also need to adjudicate if several players claim a number at the same time. At the end of the game, review the number patterns of the relevant times tables. How do we know to which number 'family' a number belongs? How do you know a 2s number when you see it? (It is an even number; it is a number ending in 2, 4, 6, 8, 0.) Ask the same for the 5s and 10s.

GAME VARIATION

• The game can be simplified by including only products of 2×, 5× and 10× in the bag.
• Extend the game by including 3× and 4× tables (as in Level B of the Scottish 5–14 Guidelines).

MULTIPLES STAND UP

TEACHING CONTENT

☆ Counting orally (N: 2a; MD: B).
☆ Recognising patterns of multiples (N: 3b; MD: B).

HOW TO PLAY

This game can be played with a small group or the whole class. Ask the group to sit in a circle. Name a particular multiplication table, say the 3× table, and choose someone to start counting at 1. The players then continue in sequence. When a player calls a multiple of the selected number, he or she must kneel up. Play continues with the next player starting where the previous one left off. Each time a multiple is called, that player kneels up. If a player who is already kneeling calls a multiple, he or she stands up and is the winner. If a child who calls a multiple does not kneel or stand, the first child to call 'multiple' is entitled to make the move.

TEACHER'S ROLE

Careful observation will enable detection of those children who are having difficulty with particular multiplication tables. If some children appear to be having difficulty with picking up the counting sequence, let them play a simpler version of the game, adapting it for their particular needs.

GAME VARIATIONS

This game has infinite variations. It can be made into a simple counting game, practising numbers from 1 to 10 only (every time 10 is reached that child kneels and counting begins again at 1, until only one child is standing). Or children can be asked to count in twos or threes and asked to kneel when, say, a number ending in 6 is called.

MATHS 1 GAMES

KEY STAGE ONE

Photocopiable games

COIN FLOWERS

TEACHING CONTENT

★ Practising sorting and matching skills (N: 5a; IH: A)
★ Recognising and handling coins (N: 1c; M: B)
★ Developing the concept of recording (N: 5b; IH: A)

PREPARATION

Assembling the game: Make four game boards by photocopying sheet 28 twice on to card (or mount on to card after copying). Colour the flowers and cover the board with clear adhesive plastic if you wish. A coin dice can be made by sticking labels on each face of a standard dice and writing on the values 1p, 2p, 5p, 10p, 20p and 50p, but it is more fun for the children if you create a giant dice from a play brick, covered with card coin labels. Use a plastic plant pot for the shaker.

Introducing the game: To ensure that the children are familiar with the different coins, give them a box full of assorted toy coins and let them sort them into values: 1p, 2p, 5p, 10p, 20p, 50p and £1. Can they tell you what the coins are called? Although the basic game requires only that they recognise and match coins, it provides an ideal opportunity to introduce names and values.

HOW TO PLAY

This is a game for two to four players. Each player chooses a coin flower game board. The players take it in turns to throw the dice. If the dice shows the same coin value as one of the empty coin spaces on the petals of a player's gameboard, she can take one of those coins and cover the coin space with it. If the dice shows a coin value that is already covered, no move can be made and it is the next player's turn. The first player to cover all six petals can take a £1 coin to cover the centre of her flower, and wins. Let the children play on for second, third and fourth places.

TEACHER'S ROLE

Although this appears a very simple game, it requires the children to match the throw of the dice to both their board and the coins in the box. If any children are having difficulty with this, let them have additional practice matching only the dice throw to the coins in the box. With children who have developed matching skills, help them move from recognition of the different coins to an understanding of their values. During the game ask: How many coins have you got? Can you say what the number is on each one? What is each of the coins called? With children who have begun to do simple addition, use two coins from 1p, 2p, 5p, and 10p only and ask: How much are these coins added together? How many different ways can you make 5p from 1p and 2p coins?

GAME VARIATIONS

The game can be made more difficult by altering the game boards so that they show just the coin values (rather than the coin images). The coin dice for this game can then be amended to show just the coin values rather than the shapes of the coins themselves.

HOW TO PLAY COIN FLOWERS

For 2 to 4 players

YOU NEED: a coin flower game board for each player, a box or play till of coins, a coin dice and shaker.

❶ Each player should choose a coin flower game board.

❷ Take it in turns to throw the dice. On your throw, if the dice shows the same coin value as one of the empty coin spaces on the petals of your game board, you can take one of those coins and cover the coin space with it. If the dice shows a coin that is already covered, no move can be made and it is the next player's turn.

❸ The first player to cover all six petals can take a £1 coin to cover the centre of her flower, and wins.

❹ Play on to see who comes 2nd, 3rd and 4th.

COIN FLOWER GAME BOARDS

Cut out to make individual game boards.

COLOUR CATERPILLAR

TEACHING CONTENT

☆ Exploring patterns and recognising sequences (N: 2a; PS: A)

☆ Create repeating patterns to develop ideas of regularity and sequencing (N: 3a; IH: A)

PREPARATION

Assembling the game: A colour dice is needed for this game. This can be made by covering the faces of a building block or standard dice with sticky labels, each indicating one of six colours – red, blue, yellow, green, brown and purple, for example.

Introducing the game: Show the children pictures of brightly-coloured caterpillars to stimulate interest. Can they see the different segments? Have they seen caterpillars in real life? Do they know what they grow into? Dance and movement activities, and Eric Carle's book *The Very Hungry Caterpillar*, are other ways of introducing the theme.

HOW TO PLAY

This is a game for two or more players. The teacher and each player needs a copy of photocopiable sheet 31 and a set of coloured crayons in the six colours shown on the dice. To begin, the teacher provides the model by colouring in the segments of a caterpillar in the six colours, in a sequence of her own choosing. The players must then try to replicate this colour sequence, in order, on their own caterpillar. They take turns to throw the dice; when they throw the colour shown on the next segment in the sequence, they can colour in that segment on their own caterpillar. Emphasise that they can only colour in a segment if they have coloured in the segment immediately before it – otherwise their throw does not count. The first player to colour in the tail (the last segment) is the winner.

TEACHER'S ROLE

There is no 'How to play' sheet as such for this game, as the colour caterpillar template can be used for several purposes. The teacher should direct the children as necessary. Once the game is over, the teacher can use the colour caterpillar to make repeating patterns. Specify the number of times that the sequence should be repeated. Make 30 individual colour cards in the six colours on the dice (five in each colour). Deal out a set of cards to each child and ask them to replicate a colour sequence on the caterpillar. When the children have done this, tell them to lay their sequences end to end to create a repeating pattern. Can they see where each sequence begins and ends? The cards can be used for other sequencing activities.

GAME VARIATIONS

The colour caterpillar can be used to concentrate more closely on sequencing skills. A repeating sequence could be used – for example: red, blue, yellow, red, blue, yellow – and the dice could be restricted to these three colours (the same colour on opposite faces). Progressive patterns could be introduced: one red, two blues, three yellows, four greens and so on. Stick caterpillars together to give longer sequence possibilities, and reduce on the photocopier if you wish to retain an A4 size.

EXTENSIONS

★ Classifying, representing and interpreting data (N: 5a, b; IH: B)

The colour caterpillar game can be used as the basis for a simple data handling activity for the whole class. Each child is given a colour caterpillar. A two-colour dice is needed (three faces in each colour). The children then throw the dice six times and colour in their caterpillar to show the order of the colours thrown. Rather than taking turns to throw the dice, as in the game, it may be easier if children fill in their caterpillars individually or in small groups – this could take place over the duration of a morning or a whole day if necessary, in order to minimise disruption. Once this is done, the children can count how many segments of each colour they each have on their caterpillar. Can they find others with the same totals and sort themselves into groups accordingly? They can then make a caterpillar pictogram to show all the different totals (as shown on the left). This will have to be done as a wall chart to accommodate all of the caterpillars. Make sure that the children place each caterpillar in the correct column. Which totals were the most common? How many different possible sequences are there with two colours? Increase the variation by playing with a three-colour dice (opposite faces in the same colour). Compare the number of sequences these allow. At a slightly more advanced level, the children could look at the colour sequences in each column. Are any the same? How many different possible sequences are there with two colours?

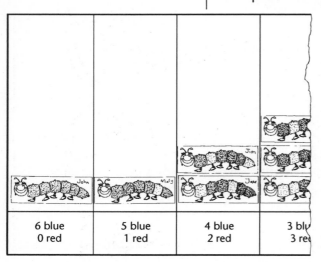

6 blue 0 red	5 blue 1 red	4 blue 2 red	3 blue 3 red

★ Classifying, representing and interpreting data (N: 5a, b; IH: B)
★ Developing mental methods for adding (N: 3d; AS: B)
★ Using a calculator (N: 1d, 3e; AS: B)

This game can be played with the emphasis on number rather than on colour, in a similar way to the extension above. All of the children in the class need a 'number' caterpillar of their own. They then throw a 1 to 6 dice and write down the first six numbers they throw, in order, on the segments of their caterpillar. When this is done, they can add up the values (using a calculator if necessary) to find the total score of their caterpillar. Can they find others with the same total and sort themselves into groups accordingly? They can then make a caterpillar pictogram to show all the different totals. This will have to be done as a wall chart to accommodate all of the caterpillars. Check that the children place each caterpillar in the correct column. Which totals were the most common? Did caterpillars with the same total all have the same set of numbers in their sequence? How many different ways were there to make up the same total? Can they find any other ways? Was the same number sequence thrown more than once?

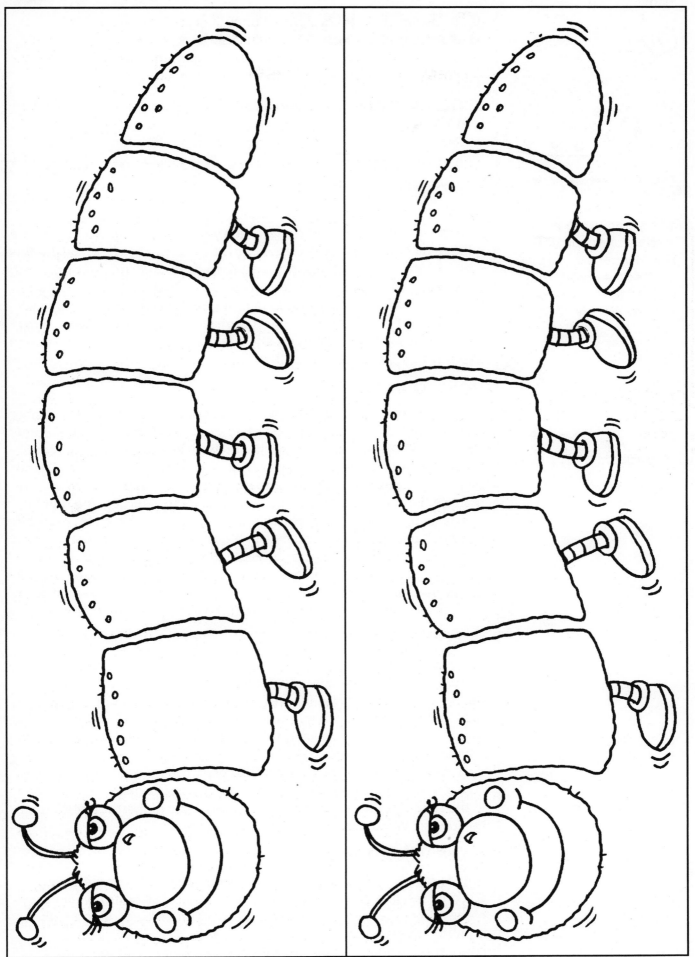

PHOTOCOPIABLE SHEETS
1 to 10 number cards sheet 33.
FOR CONSTRUCTION
Thin card, scissors, adhesive.
FOR PLAYING
*A set of 1 to 10 number cards
per player plus two additional
sets, a bag.*

BAG OF TEN

TEACHING CONTENT

☆ Knowing number names and understanding number values from 1 to 10 (N: 2a, b; RTN: A)
☆ Recognising sequences, including odd and even numbers, with numbers up to 10 (N: 2b; PS: A)

PREPARATION

Assembling the game: Copy, or mount, photocopiable sheet 33 on to card. It can then be cut up to make individual number cards. You can use either digit or dot number cards. A bag is then needed to hold the number cards, so that the players cannot see which cards they are drawing.
Introducing the game: This game operates on the same principle as a lucky dip. Perhaps as an introduction, the children could play a game of lucky dip and try to predict each time what number will be drawn. How often do they guess correctly? Is any one number drawn more often than the others? What does this tell them?

HOW TO PLAY

This is a game for two or more players. A complete set of 1 to 10 number cards is needed for each player, plus two extra sets. Place all of the number cards in the bag. To start, the teacher draws a few cards (five, say) from the bag and then lays them out to create a number sequence. Shake the bag before each card is drawn, and encourage the children to follow this practice during the game. The players must try to duplicate the number sequence by drawing number cards, in turn, from the bag. This must be done by building up the sequence in order: if a number is drawn that is part of the sequence, it cannot be kept unless the player has all of the numbers earlier in the sequence. If the number drawn cannot be used, it is returned to the bag and play continues. The first player to get all of the cards in the number sequence, in the correct order, is the winner.

TEACHER'S ROLE

While the game is in progress, encourage the children to look at each number they draw. What number is it? Is it a part of the sequence? Is it the next number in the sequence? Help them to understand the logic behind the game – which numbers they can use and why – and use this to build upon their sequencing skills. The target sequence is random, so it will not be in any particular order. To develop number sequencing skills, play a sorting game: take turns to draw five numbers from the bag and arrange them in ascending/descending order. Look at the numbers in the sequence. What is their total? Who has the highest total? Who has the lowest? What is the difference between them?

GAME VARIATIONS

Instead of a random sequence, a more structured number sequence could be set: in ascending order from 1 to 10 or starting from a number higher along the number line; in descending order from 10 or a higher number; repeating sequences, such as 1, 1, 2, 2, 3, 3 and so on. You could also introduce sequences with constant or cumulative jumps.

1 TO 10 NUMBER CARDS

5	10	5	10	5	10	5	10
4	9	4	9	4	9	4	9
3	8	3	8	3	8	3	8
2	7	2	7	2	7	2	7
1	6	1	6	1	6	1	6

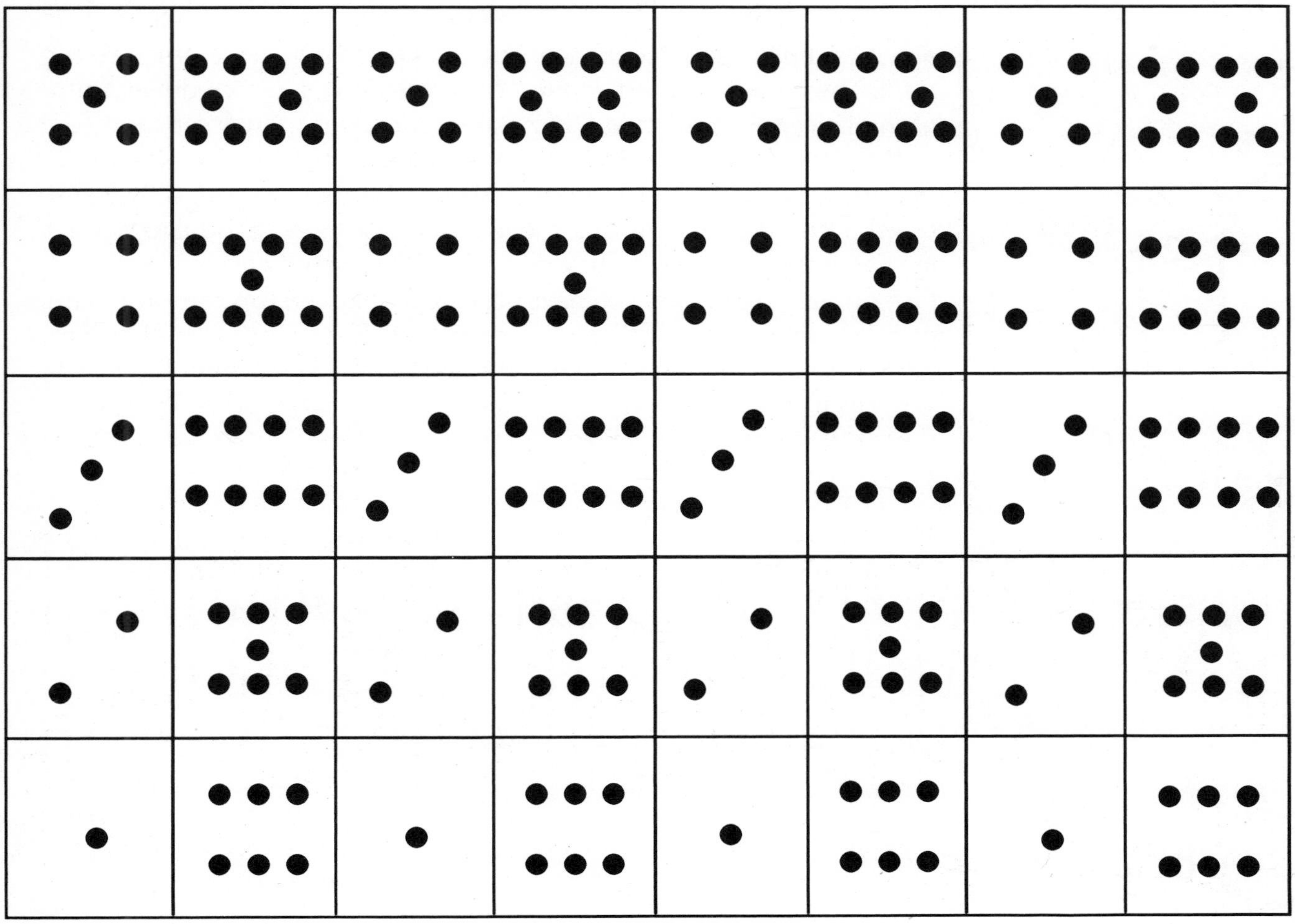

CLOTHES LINE

TEACHING CONTENT

☆ Recognising patterns and sequences (N: 3a; PS: A)

PREPARATION

Assembling the game: Make a miniature clothes line as shown in the illustration below. Colouring one of the poles on the clothes line blue and the other red will make reference easier when describing positions of clothes on the line. You will need one copy of the clothes cards sheet per player, plus one extra set of cards to use as playing cards. Cut up the sheets to make individual cards. Cut up another sheet of clothes cards and fold over the top edge of each card so that they can be 'hung' on the clothes line. If you colour in the cards, make sure all sets are identical to avoid confusion – all shirts are red, all vests are yellow and so on.

Introducing the game: Even though some homes no longer have clothes lines as such, children will have seen clothes lines in pictures and have used the same procedure in classroom displays.

HOW TO PLAY

This is a game for two to four players. One complete set of clothes cards is needed per player, plus one extra set. The teacher sets up the clothes line and chooses ten cards, each showing a different item of clothing, then shuffles them and turns over the first seven cards. The corresponding cards from the set that have been folded are hung on the line *in the order that they were drawn* to serve as the target sequence. The aim is to replicate this sequence. The ten cards are then returned to the pack. The pack is shuffled and the cards are dealt out, face down, until each player has seven cards. The players must not show their cards to the others. The rest of the pack is placed face down in the middle. The players then take turns to turn over the top card of the pile. If they wish to keep the card, they must remove a card from their hand and place it face up beside the pile. If they do not wish to keep the card, they place it face up beside the pile. The next player can take the top card from either pile. No player is allowed to keep more than seven cards in his hand at a time. Play continues in this way until one of the players has the same cards as the sequence on the clothes line. To win, the player must lay them out *in the same order* as the target sequence. The rest of the players

fold

dowelling

Plasticine

check that the cards are laid out in the correct sequence. If a mistake is made, that player is out of the game and all of his cards are returned to the pack. Play continues until the sequence is replicated correctly. If all of the cards are turned over and no-one has won, restart the game with a new clothes line sequence or, if the players wish, reshuffle the pack and continue playing.

vest	towel	shirt	socks
vest	towel	socks	shirt
vest	socks	towel	shirt

TEACHER'S ROLE

As the game is being played, it will be helpful if the teacher moves around the group of players to assist them in sequencing their cards. Holding the cards in sequence as they are collected will make it easier to check which cards are still required. Help the players to understand that the sequence is important – having the same cards is not enough, they must be in the same order to form a matching sequence. If the children have difficulty holding all of the cards in one hand at the same time, they could make small stands (like those used in Scrabble) to hold them, or even lay them out face up on the table top – at early levels, the children will be concentrating on their own cards rather than those of others. One way to develop sequencing skills is to choose a restricted number of cards (four or five, say) and look at the variations of sequences these cards offer. Can the children make sequences in which the same clothes are in different ordinal positions each time? Try placing the same card at the beginning of the line each time, but varying the cards that follow as shown in the illustration. Can the children appreciate that these are all different sequences? Try with the same card at the end of the line, but varying the earlier cards. Children can record the sequences in picture form.

GAME VARIATIONS

Although not as much fun, the game works equally well without the 3-D clothes line. However, the teacher will need to place the target sequence in full view of all the players. To extend the game to a sequence of ten cards, lay out the sequence; but instead of having cards dealt out to them, the players take turns to turn over the top card of the pack and place matching cards underneath the corresponding sequence card. However, cards can only be matched in order, so if the clothes cards earlier in the sequence have not been matched a card cannot be used. Cards that cannot be matched are placed face up beside the pile and, if all of the cards in the pile are turned over, these cards are then turned over to provide a new pile to draw from. You can, of course, reduce the number of cards in the sequence to make the game easier. The player to lay out the last card in the sequence is the winner.

HOW TO PLAY CLOTHES LINE

For 2 to 4 players

YOU NEED: a 'clothes line', a set of 'clothes' cards per player plus one extra set of cards, and a set of clothes cards to hang on the clothes line.

❶ Choose 10 cards showing different items of clothing. Shuffle them, then turn over the top 7 cards and lay them out in order to form the target sequence.

❷ Hang this sequence of clothes on the line, using the folded set of cards, so that all the players can see them. Players must try to copy this sequence.

❸ Return the 10 cards to the pack. Shuffle the pack and deal out 7 cards to each player. (Do not let the other players see them.)

❹ Place the pack face down in the middle.

❺ The first player to go turns over the top card.

If he wishes to keep it, he must take another card from his hand and place it, face up, beside the pack.

If he does not wish to keep it he can simply place it, face up, beside the pack.

No player can have more than 7 cards at a time.

❻ The next player can take the top card from either pile.

❼ Players take turns to draw cards in this way.

❽ The first player to collect all of the clothes on the line and lay them out in the correct sequence is the winner.

CLOTHES CARDS
Colour and cut out to make individual cards.

vest	pillow case	socks	trousers
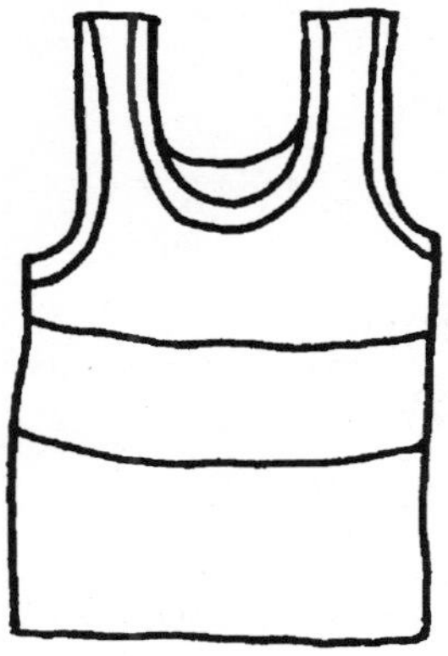			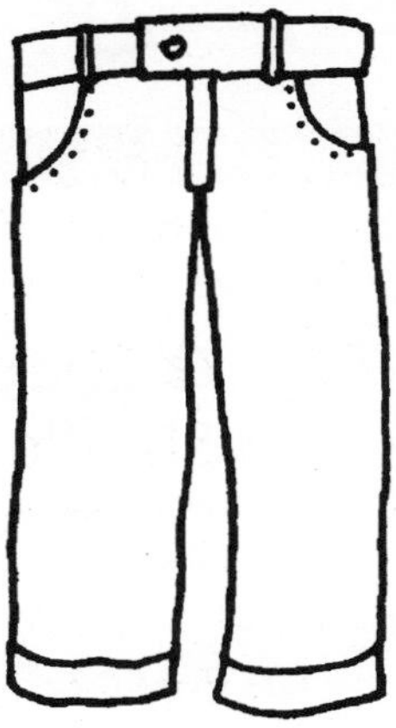
skirt	towel	shirt	pants
	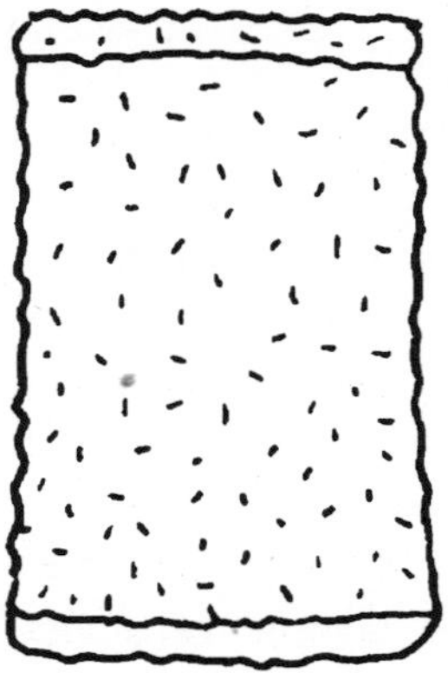		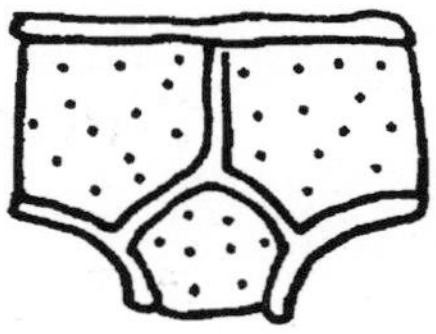
tights 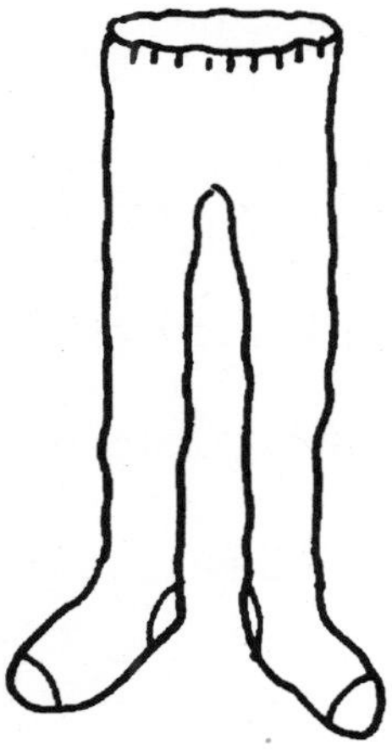	dress 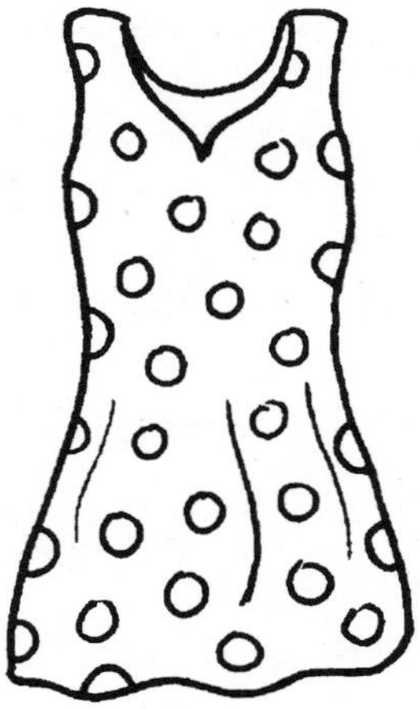	jumper 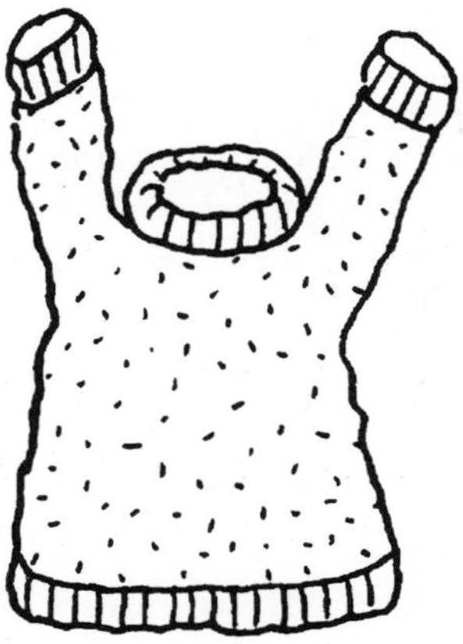	sheet 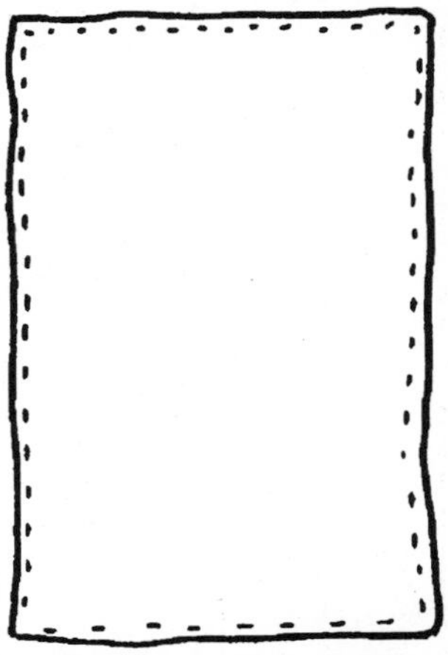

BUS STOP

TEACHING CONTENT

☆ Counting to 5, knowing number names (both ordinal and cardinal) (N: 2a; RTN: A)
☆ Adding and subtracting numbers to 5 (N: 3b; AS: A)
☆ Understanding that subtraction is the inverse of addition (N: 3d; AS: A)

PREPARATION

Assembling the game: See diagrams on page 39. Photocopying, or mounting, the bus, bus stop and passengers (photocopiable pages 41, 42 and 40) on to card will make the pieces more sturdy and give them a longer life. The pieces can be coloured in with crayons to make them look more attractive. Make sure, when adding staples to the bus and bus stop, that they are in the correct position (indicated by the black squares); otherwise the passengers will not fit into the pockets.

Introducing the game: Most of the children will have been on bus journeys or, at least, will have seen buses and people waiting at bus stops. Indeed, orderly queuing will form a part of their everyday life at school. Can the children say why orderly queuing is a good thing? What would happen if people did not queue properly?

HOW TO PLAY

This is a game for two or more players. The aim of the game is to move the passenger cards from the bus stop on to the bus itself. To start, place all of the passengers into the pockets on the bus stop. All of the players use the same bus stop and bus, and take turns to roll the dice. The first player to roll a one can move the first passenger on to the bus. Play continues and the passengers are moved in numerical order, one by one, on to the bus. Any throw higher or less than the position of the next passenger in the queue does not count. The player who throws a five and moves the last passenger on to the bus is the winner. If a player throws a six, she can take another turn at throwing the dice.

TEACHER'S ROLE

Discuss the passengers in the queue to demonstrate the relationship between cardinal and ordinal numbers (how 1 = the first person, 2 = the second and so on). Who is the first person in the queue? Who is the second? And so on. It is important that the children have some understanding of this before playing the game. Observe how the children place the passengers on the bus. Do they follow the ordinal order of the queue, i.e. the first passenger in the first window, the second in the second, and so on? If they do not do this, does it affect the number of passengers on the bus? Can they name the positions of the passengers on the bus? As the game progresses, ask questions to draw the children's attention to the inverse relationship between addition and subtraction. How many passengers are there on the bus and at the bus stop after each turn? Can the children predict what it will be next turn? Look at number bonds to 5, as this is a vital part of how our number system (based on 10) works. Tallying and counting on fingers are both based on units of five.

GAME VARIATIONS

• Play the game (without the bus stop) in reverse, with the passengers leaving the bus one by one to go home. The first player to throw 1 picks a passenger to leave the bus. Point out that the passengers do not necessarily leave in numerical order. The children can decide which passenger leaves next. In this way, they can see that the first on is not necessarily the first off. The first player to throw a 5 and remove the last passenger is the winner. Can the children understand why the orders for getting on and getting off the bus might be different?

• The number of passengers and spaces could be increased to 10, and number cards in a bag or a 1 to 10 spinner could be used to extend the number bonds in this activity.

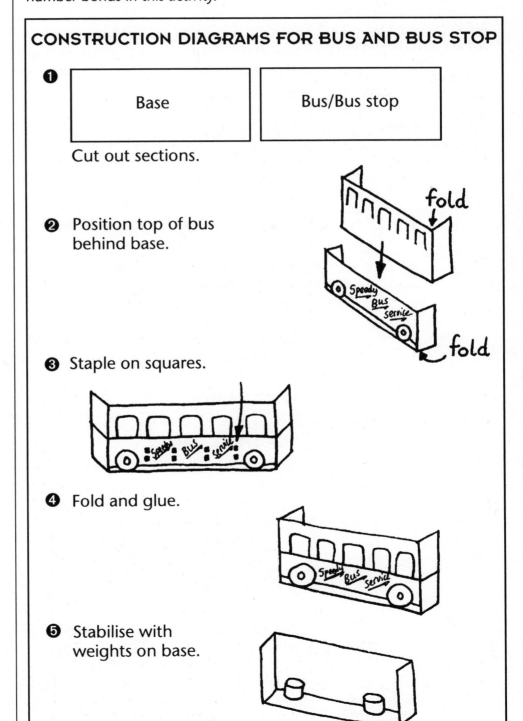

CONSTRUCTION DIAGRAMS FOR BUS AND BUS STOP

❶ Base | Bus/Bus stop

Cut out sections.

❷ Position top of bus behind base.

fold

Speedy Bus service

fold

❸ Staple on squares.

Speedy Bus service

❹ Fold and glue.

Speedy Bus service

❺ Stabilise with weights on base.

HOW TO PLAY BUS STOP

For 2 or more players

YOU NEED: the bus stop and bus boards, 5 passenger cards, a dice and shaker.

The aim of the game is to move the passengers, in order, from the bus stop queue on to the bus.

All players use the same bus stop, bus and passengers.

❶ Take turns to throw the dice.

❷ The first player to throw a 1 can move the first passenger from the bus stop on to the bus. Any other score does not count, and play continues.

If a player throws a 6, he gets another turn.

❸ The next player to throw a 2 can move the second passenger card from the bus stop on to the bus.

❹ Continue playing, moving each of the passengers in order on to the bus.

❺ The first player to throw a five for the final passenger and move him/her on to the bus is the winner.

✂ -

PLAYING PIECES

Colour and cut out.

GAMES

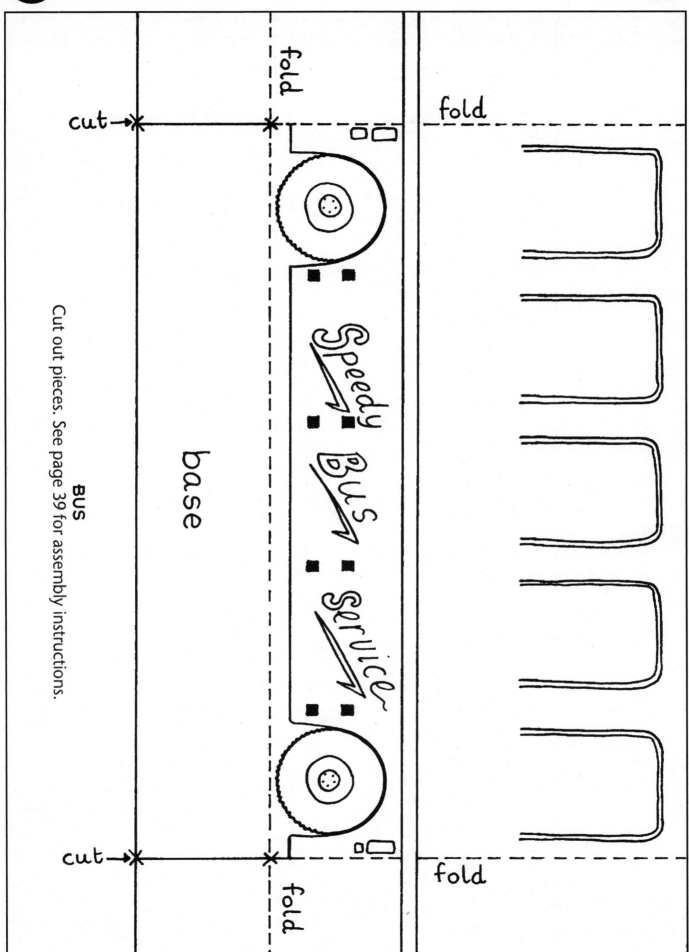

cut →

fold

fold

cut →

fold

fold

base

BUS
Cut out pieces. See page 39 for assembly instructions.

Speedy Bus Service

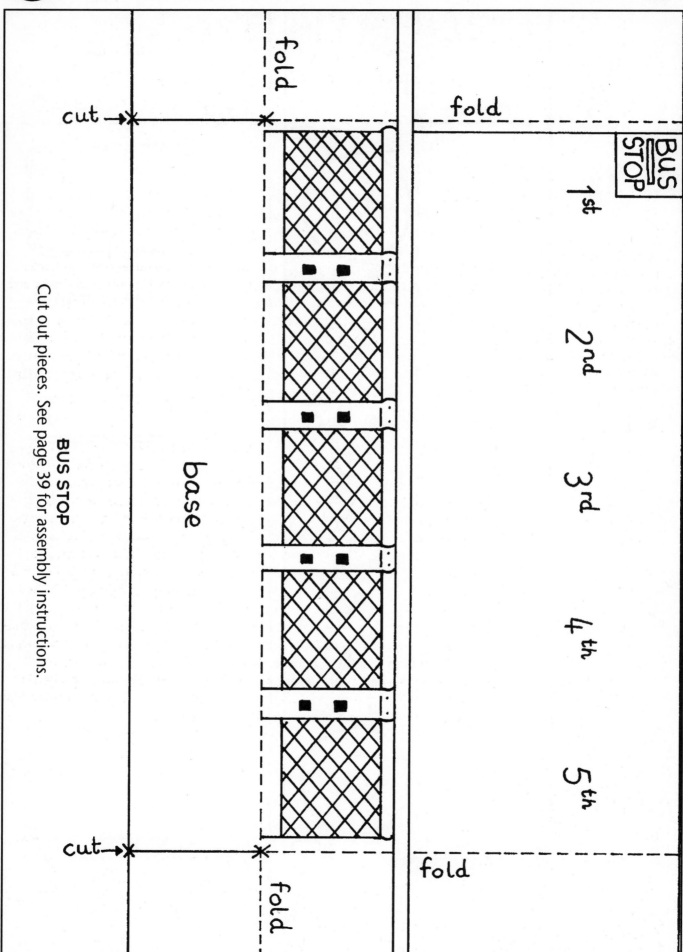

BUS STOP

Cut out pieces. See page 39 for assembly instructions.

fold

cut

base

fold

cut

fold

BUS STOP

1st 2nd 3rd 4th 5th

fold

IDENTIKIT

TEACHING CONTENT

☆ Counting collections of objects, checking the total (N: 2a; RTN: A)
☆ Practising number bonds of 10 (N: 3c, 4a; AS: A, B)
☆ Exploring patterns in addition and subtraction (N: 3b; AS: A)

WHAT YOU NEED

PHOTOCOPIABLE SHEETS
Identikit game board and facial features cards sheet 46, 'How to play' sheet 45 and 1 to 10 number cards sheet 33.

FOR CONSTRUCTION
Thin card, scissors, adhesive.

FOR PLAYING
An Identikit board for each player, 'How to play' sheet, two sets of 1 to 10 number cards per player and a set of facial features cards for each player, a bag.

PREPARATION

Assembling the game: Photocopy, or mount, the 1 to 10 number cards (page 33) on to card and cut out the individual cards. You can use either the digits or the dots cards. Two sets of cards are needed for each player. Using card rather than paper for the Identikit game board and facial features will also prolong the life of the game. The facial features cards need to be cut out so that they can be placed individually on to the board.
Introducing the game: The children may have seen police identikit or photofit pictures on the television news or in a newspaper. Perhaps you could provide a range of facial features and allow the children to make different identikit faces in order to familiarise themselves with the game. Would the police use different-shaped examples of each feature for their identikit faces? Why would this be important?

HOW TO PLAY

This is a game for two or more players. Give each player an Identikit game board, a set of 1 to 10 number cards and a set of the facial features cards. The players place a number card on each of the ten squares on their game board. The rest of the number cards are placed in the bag. The players take turns to draw cards from the bag. If the number drawn can be added to one of the cards already on their board to make a total of 10, they place the card they have drawn on top of the card on the board. So: if a 3 is drawn and one of the cards on the board is a 7, the 3 can be placed on top of the 7. The 10 square with the number 10 card will not need another card added to it: it is, in essence, a 'free' card. If the number on the card cannot be added to a number on the board to make a total of 10, the card is returned to the bag and play continues. When all of the squares of a facial feature have been covered, that player can exchange the cards for that facial feature card, which can be placed on the board. The first player to complete an Identikit face is the winner. Play continues until everyone has completed a face.

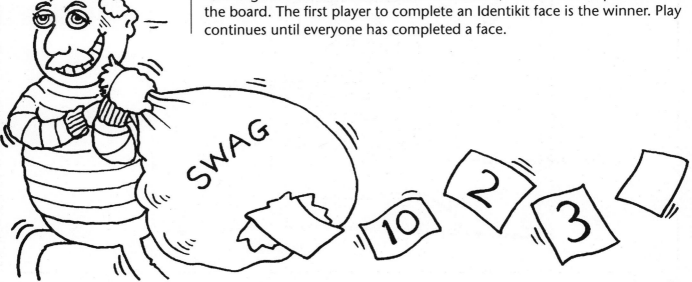

TEACHER'S ROLE

Some children may be thinking ahead to the numbers they need to draw from the bag in order to cover a square, while others may be counting on each time a card is drawn. Encourage the children's awareness of number bonds up to 10 by asking questions as the game progresses. Which numbers do they need to win the moustache card? If they cannot use the card they draw, which number would they have needed? Ask the children to write out the values of the facial features as number sentences, then add up these totals. So: for the left eye 9 + 1 = 10, for the right eye 3 + 7 = 10, for the nose 2 + 8 + 6 + 4 = 20, and so on. The total value of all the facial features is 100. Look at the different ways of making up the totals. For instance, the total for each eye is 10 but different number bonds are used.

GAME VARIATIONS

• The Identikit board could be amended so that each square has its own value: zero for the eyes, and each of the other squares represents a value from 1 to 9. In this way, all of the number bonds from 1 to 10 are covered.

• Use both the digit and the dot 1 to 10 cards to play this game, to make sure the children recognise the digit form of numbers and understand that these numbers represent a 'set' of objects. Cards with a value of 0 could be included if suitable.

HOW TO PLAY IDENTIKIT

For 2 or more players

YOU NEED: 1 to 10 number cards (two sets of number cards per player), an Identikit board and a full set of facial features per player, a bag.

❶ Each player takes a set of 1 to 10 number cards and places one on each of the ten squares on the Identikit board (in any order).

❷ Place the remaining sets of number cards in the bag.

❸ Take turns to draw number cards from the bag.

If the number drawn can be added to one of the cards on your board to make 10, place the card on top of the other card on the board.

If not, return it to the bag.

❹ When a part of the face has all of its squares covered with two number cards that add up to 10, the cards can be exchanged for that Identikit piece.

So one set of 10 is needed for an eye, but two are needed for the nose.

❺ The first player to complete the Identikit face is the winner.

☆ REMEMBER!

The 10 square that has a number 10 card on it will not need another number card.

If you draw a 10, you will not be able to add it to any card on the Identikit face.

HOW TO PLAY IDENTIKIT

IDENTIKIT GAME BOARD

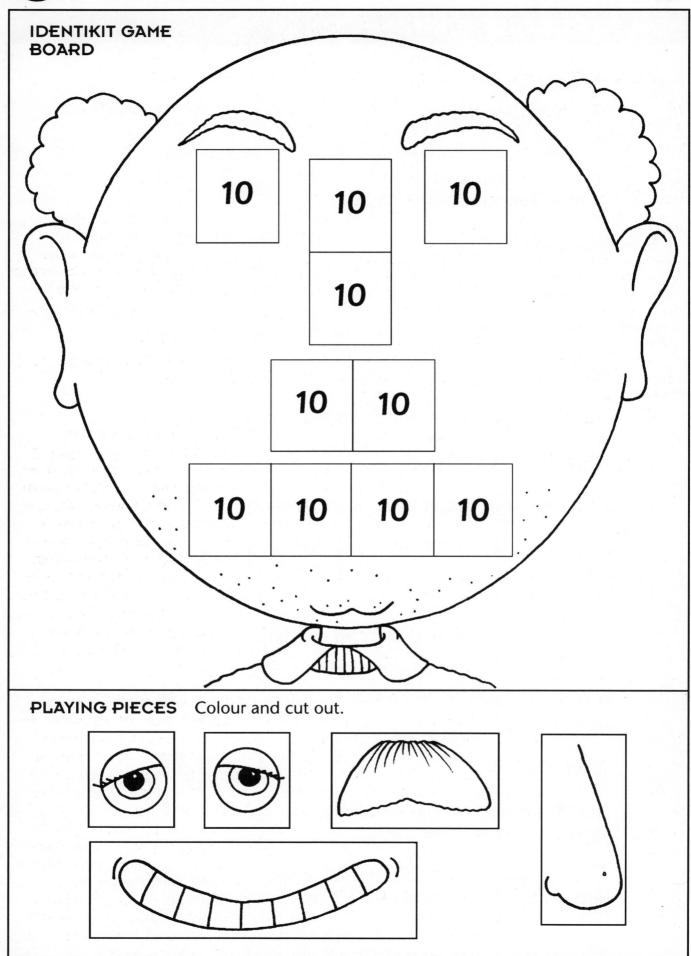

PLAYING PIECES Colour and cut out.

FIRE! FIRE!

TEACHING CONTENT

☆ Knowing number names and counting on in steps of different sizes (N: 1a, 2b; RTN: A)

☆ Exploring addition and subtraction patterns for numbers 1 to 30 (N: 3b; RTN: A, B; AS: A, B)

PREPARATION

Assembling the game: Colour each fire-engine in a different colour (red, green, blue or yellow), then colour each of the fire stations and their adjoining 'start' squares on the tracks in matching colours. Make the fire-engines, burning house and game board as shown in the 'Special section' (pages 134 and 135). The fire-engines and burning house can also be decorated to make the board more attractive. The burning house is placed at the centre of the game board.

Introducing the game: The drama of a fire-fighting scenario can be incorporated into the game. Who is in the house? How did the fire start? What will the fire-fighters do when they get there?

HOW TO PLAY

This is a game for two to four players. To start, each of the players chooses a fire engine and places it in its station (the blue fire engine in the blue fire station and so on). They then take turns to throw the dice and move the number of spaces thrown along the track. The first player to reach the hydrant in the final square is the winner. However, the exact number of spaces required at the end of the game must be thrown in order to reach the hydrant. So: if you are on square 28 and you throw a 3, the throw does not score. Continue the game until all of the players reach the hydrant on square 30. It may be necessary to demonstrate to the children how the front of the fire-engines can be used to mark their position on the track (as the engines are bigger than the individual track squares). If this presents problems, it may be simpler to use coloured counters rather than the fire-engines, though this may reduce the excitement of the game.

TEACHER'S ROLE

As the game is in progress, note which children count laboriously in ones and which are able to anticipate on which square the fire-engine will land. If it will not be too disruptive, ask the children at random which square they will land on before moving their fire-engines to encourage mental addition skills. The players can then check their estimates once they have moved. This can lead on to work on number bonds. If appropriate, you could play an example game for a group, or the whole class, using just one board and keeping a written record of each move: number of the square on which you stand (first number) + dice throw = second number. Look at the numbers involved. Which is the bigger (stress *bigger* rather than *biggest*) of the two numbers? Will the second number always be bigger than the first? Try playing the game in reverse. The order in which the players finish can be recorded on the photocopiable record sheet, reinforcing understanding of ordinal numbers.

GAME VARIATIONS

• Using a digital number dice rather than the traditional dots dice will give the game a different slant and help to identify those children who appear to know the names of numbers but are unsure of their real values.

• Look at the numbers featured on the dice. Provide three other dice with the dots drawn on sticky labels attached to the sides. On one, add an extra dot to each side of the dice. Which numbers does the dice show now? Which numbers have we lost? Add two extra dots to each face of the second dice and three extra dots to each face of the third dice. Which numbers do these dice show? Which numbers have we lost? Play the Fire! Fire! game with each of the players using a different dice. Which dice is the fastest? What problem is presented if the exact number is required at the end of the game? Use a building block if a normal dice is too small.

• The game can also be played using colour rather than number as the key factor. Cover the faces of a dice with sticky paper and colour in each of the faces differently (red, blue, green, brown, yellow and purple). Then colour each of the first six squares on the board in one of these colours and repeat the colour sequence along the rest of the track. Players move on to the next square showing the colour they have thrown each turn. This will encourage the children to look ahead and see their jumps as complete moves forward, rather than counting one by one.

• The game can also be played with the emphasis on odd and even numbers. Two of the fire engines can only move if odd numbers are thrown, and the other two only on even numbers. Of course, this version favours those players who can only move when an even number is thrown (as the even numbers total 12 while the odd numbers total 9), but a bonus start could be given to the players with the odd numbers. What number do the children think such a bonus start should be? The difficult part comes when the players are near the end and need to throw the exact number to finish.

EXTENSION

★ Exploring patterns and recognising sequences (N: 2a; PS: A, B)
★ Recording data in charts and diagrams (N: 5b; IH: A, B)

The children can use the photocopiable record sheet (page 50) to record all of their scores during the game. Encourage them to colour in the squares on the number strip using alternate colours to show their scores each round. For example: If a 2 is thrown on the first turn, then squares 1 and 2 are shaded blue; if a 4 is then thrown, squares 3 to 6 are shaded red; the third score will be shaded in blue, and so on. It may be more practical to cut out the individual number strips and give one to each player, rather than pass the sheet round each turn. When the game is over, the sequences of throws can be discussed. Are any two players' sequences the same? What is the longest sequence of one number being thrown by one player? This will help to demonstrate that any patterns are due to chance and would be unlikely to recur if another game were played. How many dice throws did the winner take? How many did the loser take?

HOW TO PLAY FIRE! FIRE!

For 2 to 4 players

YOU NEED: a dice and shaker, the Fire! Fire! game board, a fire engine (coloured in with crayons) for each player.

❶ Place the fire engines on their starting squares – the blue fire engine on the blue square, and so on.

❷ Take turns to roll the dice and move your fire engine the number of spaces thrown along your track.

❸ The first player to reach the fire hydrant on square 30 is the winner.

☆ REMEMBER!

You must throw the exact number needed to land on square 30.

So: if you are on square 28 and you roll a 3, that is too many. The throw does not score.

RECORD SHEET FOR FIRE! FIRE!

Write in the name of each player and colour in the fire engines.

Use one colour to fill in the number of spaces you move on your first turn. Use another colour to show your second turn. Change colours for each turn, so it is easy to see how many spaces you moved each time.

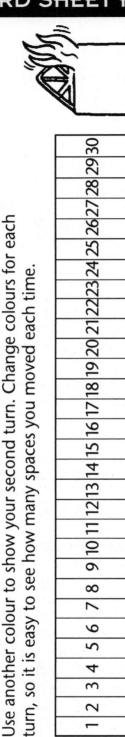

1 2 3 4 5 6 7 8 9 10 11 12 13 14 15 16 17 18 19 20 21 22 23 24 25 26 27 28 29 30

1 2 3 4 5 6 7 8 9 10 11 12 13 14 15 16 17 18 19 20 21 22 23 24 25 26 27 28 29 30

1 2 3 4 5 6 7 8 9 10 11 12 13 14 15 16 17 18 19 20 21 22 23 24 25 26 27 28 29 30

1 2 3 4 5 6 7 8 9 10 11 12 13 14 15 16 17 18 19 20 21 22 23 24 25 26 27 28 29 30

Who came 1st, 2nd, 3rd and 4th? Write in your position on the burning house at the end of your line.

 Name

 Name

 Name

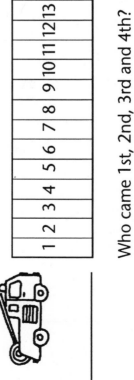 Name

WHAT YOU NEED

PHOTOCOPIABLE SHEETS
Playing track sheet 141, playing and centre pieces sheet 142, 'How to play' sheet 53, record sheets 54 and 55 (extension).

FOR CONSTRUCTION
Card 445mm × 445mm for game board, thin card, scissors, adhesive, sticky labels (optional), coloured crayons.

FOR PLAYING
A game board, a frog for each player, 'How to play' sheet, a dice and shaker, pencils and crayons.

HOP IT!

TEACHING CONTENT

★ Knowing number names and counting on in steps of different sizes (N: 1a, 2a; RTN: A)

★ Exploring addition and subtraction patterns for numbers 1 to 20 (N: 3a, 3b; RTN: A, B; AS: A, B)

PREPARATION

Assembling the game: Photocopy sheet 142 ('Special section') once. Colour in the frog playing pieces and the water lily flower, then make them as indicated. Photocopy sheet 141 ('Special section') four times and construct the game board as shown on page 135, sticking the water lily in the centre and colouring the starting stone of each individual track to match one of the frogs. The game board can be coloured further to make it more attractive. If the children have difficulty coping with larger numbers, you could make a restricted dice showing only the values 1 to 3 by covering the 4, 5 and 6 with sticky labels and drawing in the values 1 to 3 (with 1 on the opposite face to the original 1, and so on).

Introducing the game: Discuss frogs with the children. Where do frogs live? How do they move? Use frogs as the theme for dance and movement activities, incorporating their hopping movements.

HOW TO PLAY

This is a game for two to four players. Each player needs a frog playing piece, which is placed on its own starting square (the blue frog on the blue stone, and so on). The players then take turns to throw the dice and move their frog the number of spaces thrown along the track. If a player lands on one of the lily pads, she misses the next turn. The first player to reach the water lily at the centre of the board is the winner. However, the exact number must be thrown to finish. So if a player is on stone 18 and throws a 4, that throw does not score and she must wait until her next turn to try again. If you wish, let the children play on to determine the finishing position of each player. As the game is in progress, the players can use the record sheet (page 54) to record their scores, writing down the number of the stone on which they land at each turn rather than the score on the dice. At the end, they can also fill in their finishing positions on the lily pads. An alternative way to record the game is to give each player a copy of the individual playing track (photocopiable page ???). Each player then either colours in the stones on which she lands to show her position after each turn, or colours in the number of stones moved each turn using a different colour.

TEACHER'S ROLE

The children may need help in counting and recording their scores. During the game, observe whether children are counting on or are adding on their scores to determine where they will land. Ask them to predict which stone they will land on before moving to develop mental addition and number bond skills. This will all form part of the recording process. Filling in the finishing positions will introduce the use of ordinal numbers.

EXTENSION

★ Recognising and using plus and minus (N: 2c; AS: B)
★ Understanding the operations of addition and subtraction and the relationship between them (N: 3b; AS: B)

The game can be taken a step further by imposing penalties for landing on the lily pads and using record sheet 55 to chart the progress of each player during the game. This introduces a simple number line to plot movements forward (plus) and backward (minus). It is important that the children understand that 0 (zero rather than nought when using a scale) is equivalent to the starting square or a score of 0. For the sake of clarity, it might be best if forward moves are recorded in one colour and backward moves in another – arrows can also be added to show the direction of moves. The illustration below shows some examples of recording scores using the number line. The teacher should observe to what extent the children anticipate the correct landing place when adding or subtracting along the number line. Children who are confident will draw one clear curving line from the starting point to a destination point, with little hesitation. Lack of confidence is shown by drawing moves in a series of single-stone 'hops'. Draw children's attention to 'zero' as the starting point of the line.

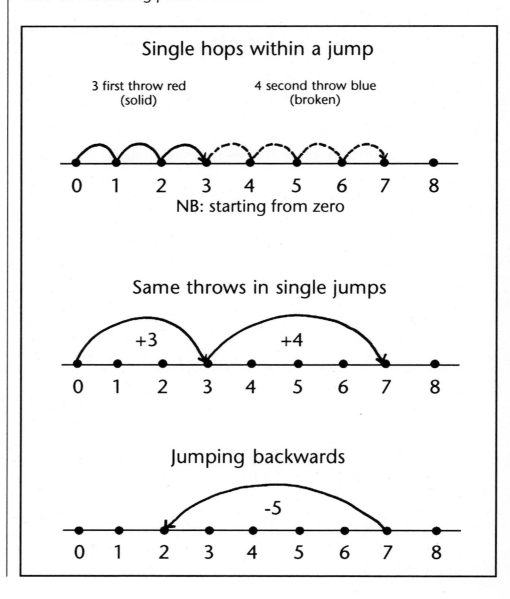

HOW TO PLAY HOP IT!

For 2 to 4 players

YOU NEED: a game board, a frog playing piece for each player, a dice and shaker, pencils and crayons.

❶ Place the frogs on the starting stones (the blue frog on the blue stone, and so on).

❷ Take turns to throw the dice and move the number of spaces thrown along the track.

❸ If you land on a lily pad, you miss a turn the next round.

❹ The first player to land on the water lily in the centre of the board is the winner.

☆ REMEMBER!

You must throw the exact number needed to move on to the water lily.

The water lily counts as 21.

So if you are on stone 20, you must throw a 1. Any other score does not let you move.

RECORD SHEET FOR HOP IT!

Write down the number of every stone you land on.

Name _____

Name _____

Name _____

Name _____

Who came 1st, 2nd, 3rd and 4th?
Write your positions in the circle on your frog.

red

blue

yellow

green

GAMES

RECORD SHEET FOR HOP IT!

Draw in each move you make on your number line.

Name _____

21

0 1 2 3 4 5 6 7 8 9 10 11 12 13 14 15 16 17 18 19 20

red

Name _____

21

0 1 2 3 4 5 6 7 8 9 10 11 12 13 14 15 16 17 18 19 20

blue

Name _____

21

0 1 2 3 4 5 6 7 8 9 10 11 12 13 14 15 16 17 18 19 20

yellow

Name _____

21

0 1 2 3 4 5 6 7 8 9 10 11 12 13 14 15 16 17 18 19 20

green

Who came 1st, 2nd, 3rd and 4th?
Write in your position on the small lily pad at the end of your line.

TO BUY A FAT PIG

TEACHING CONTENT

★ Knowing number names and counting on in steps of different sizes (N: 1a, 2a; RTN: A)

★ Addition and subtraction with numbers up to 20 (N: 3c, 3d, 4a; AS: B)

PREPARATION

Assembling the game: Photocopy sheet 144 ('Special section') twice and sheet 59 once; then make the fence enclosure for the market, the four Land Rovers and 16 pigs as indicated. Photocopy sheet 143 ('Special section') four times and construct the game board with the fenced central area as shown on page 135. Colour the Land Rovers each in a different colour, and each of the farms on the game board in matching colours. The details of the game board and Land Rovers can be coloured in to make them more attractive.

Introducing the game: Discuss the context of this game with the children, i.e. farmers going to a market to buy their livestock. The counting rhyme "There once was a sow' or traditional rhymes such as 'To market, to market' can also be used to set the scene for this activity.

HOW TO PLAY

This is a game for two to four players. All of the pigs are placed inside the market fence at the centre of the game board. To start, each player chooses a Land Rover and places it on the 'start' square of its farm parking space (shaded squares) – the blue Land Rover on the blue farm, and so on. She then places nine £1 coins on the circles next to her farm. The players take turns to throw the dice, moving their Land Rover the number of spaces thrown along the track. When they reach any of the market parking spaces (shaded squares), they can buy a pig – placing one of their £1 coins in the market square and one of the pigs in their Land Rover.

The players then continue round their track until they reach any of the farm parking spaces, where they can unload the pig into their farm pen. There are six shaded parking spaces for the farm and six for the market, to ensure that the players land on a 'farm' and a 'market' square each time round (in this simple version of the game, only one pig can be bought on each circuit). Continue playing until all of the pigs are sold. When the last pig is bought, play stops immediately and the players count up how many pigs they each have. Don't forget to count all the pigs still in Land Rovers on the track. The player with the most pigs is the winner. As the Land Rovers are larger than the track squares, it is important that the children all mark their positions on the board accurately, placing the front of the vehicle on the square they have reached.

WHAT YOU NEED

PHOTOCOPIABLE SHEETS
Playing track sheet 143, playing and centre pieces sheet 144, pigs sheet 59, 'How to play' sheet 58.

FOR CONSTRUCTION
Card 445mm × 445mm for game board, thin card, scissors, adhesive, coloured pens or crayons.

FOR PLAYING
Game board, 1 Land Rover per player, 'How to play' sheet, 16 pigs, 36 toy £1 coins, a dice and shaker.

TEACHER'S ROLE

During the game, draw the players' attention to how many pigs they each have and how many are still in the market. What is the total number of pigs that has been bought? Who has the least/most pigs at the moment? Ask about the coins. How many do you have left? How many have you spent? Use the numbers on the board to develop number awareness. Which number are you on? Which number will you be on after your next move? How many more squares are there before you reach the market/farm? Which numbers do you need to get there? Look at the relationship between the movements of the pigs and the coins. Can the children begin to see the inverse relationship? The more coins you have the fewer pigs you have, and vice versa. At the end of the game discuss the players' totals of coins and pigs – use the word 'all' alongside 'total' to help the children understand its meaning. How much money did each farm start with? How much did each farm spend? Write this out in number sentences. How much money is there in the market at the end? Write a number sentence to show how the money spent by the players adds up to make this amount.

GAME VARIATIONS

• A simple step forward is to allow more than one pig to be bought each round (if the Land Rover lands on more than one market parking space, i.e. if the player is already on a market parking space and throws a low number to land on the market parking spaces a second time). In this case, she will need to spend another £1 coin from her farm supply. If a player spends all of the money in her farm, she is the winner.

• The corner squares could be used as penalty squares – either by using prepared penalty cards or by writing the penalties on these squares before playing. Penalties might include: Traffic jam in town – miss a turn; Animals on the road – miss a turn; Go to the garage for petrol – miss two turns; Road is flooded – miss two turns; and so on.

Traffic jam in town

Miss a turn

Road is flooded

Miss two turns

Animals on the road

Miss a turn

Go to the garage
for petrol

Miss two turns

HOW TO PLAY TO BUY A FAT PIG

For 2 to 4 players

YOU NEED: a game board, 16 pigs, a Land Rover for each player, nine £1 coins for each player, a dice and shaker.

❶ Place all of the pigs in the market square and the Land Rovers on the 'start' square for each farm.

❷ Take nine £1 coins and place them on the circles next to each farm.

❸ Take turns to throw the dice and move your Land Rover the number of spaces thrown around the track.

❹ When you reach any of the market parking spaces (the shaded squares), buy a pig with one of your £1 coins. Put the coin in the market square and place the pig in your Land Rover.

❺ Continue around the track. When your Land Rover reaches any of the farm parking spaces (the shaded squares), place the pig in the farm pen.

❻ Continue playing in this way until all of the pigs have been sold.

❼ The player with the most pigs at the end of the game is the winner.

GAMES

PLAYING PIECES

Colour, cut out, glue and hold.

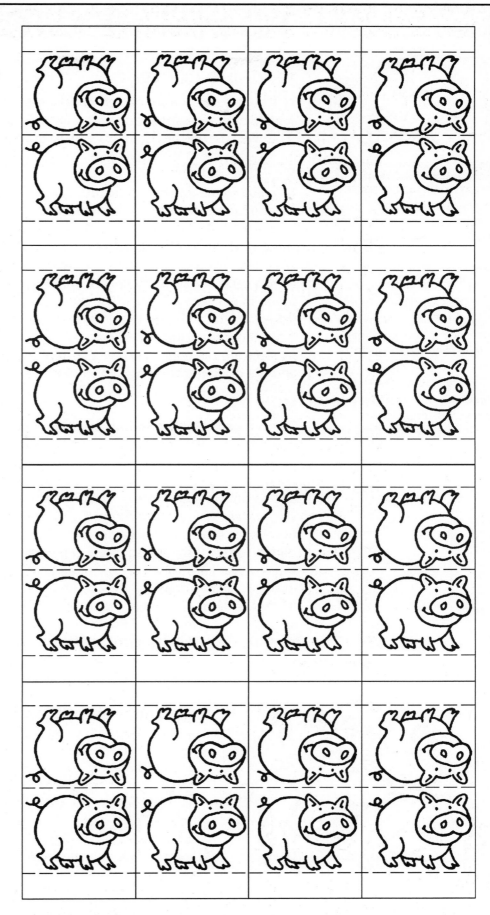

TO MARKET, TO MARKET

PHOTOCOPIABLE SHEETS
*Playing track sheet 143, playing
and centre pieces sheet 144,
animal cards and number tiles
sheet 63, 'How to play' sheet 62,
record sheets 64, 65 and 66
(extension).*

FOR CONSTRUCTION
*Card 445mm × 445mm for
game board, thin card, scissors,
adhesive, coloured pens or
crayons.*

FOR PLAYING
*Game board, 1 Land Rover per
player, 'How to play' sheet, a set
of 1 to 10 animal cards, a set of
1 to 10 number tiles and a bag,
36 toy £1 coins, a dice and
shaker.*

TEACHING CONTENT

☆ Count collections of objects checking the total (N: 2a; RTN: A)
☆ Addition and subtraction with numbers up to 30 (N: 3c, 3d, 4a; AS: B)
☆ Collect and record data in a variety of ways (N: 1e, 5b; IH:C)

PREPARATION

Assembling the game: Photocopy sheet 144 ('Special section') twice and
sheet 63 once, then make the fence enclosure for the market, the four
Land Rovers, the ten animal cards and the ten number cards. Photocopy
sheet 143 ('Special section') four times and construct the game board
with the fenced central area as shown on page 135. Colour the Land
Rovers each in a different colour, and each of the farms on the game
board in matching colours. The details of the game board and Land
Rovers can be coloured in to make them more attractive. Place the set of
1 to 10 number cards in the bag.

Introducing the game: 'To buy a fat pig' (page 56) uses the same board
and is a good introductory activity for this game.

HOW TO PLAY

This is a game for two to four players. All of the animal cards are placed
inside the market fence at the centre of the game board. To start, each
player chooses a Land Rover and places it on the 'start' square of its farm
parking space (shaded squares) – the blue Land Rover on the blue farm,
and so on. He then places nine £1 coins on the circles next to his farm.
The players take turns to throw the dice and move their Land Rover the
number of spaces thrown along the track. When they reach the market
parking spaces (shaded squares), they draw a number card from the bag
– this determines which set of animals can be bought at the market. For
example, if they draw a 7 they can buy the 7 turkeys. They take a £1 coin
from their farm, place it in the market square and place the 7 turkeys in
their Land Rover (each set of animals costs £1). The
number cards are returned to the bag each time. If a
player draws the number for an animal card that has
already been sold, the player stays put until his next turn
and then picks another card. The players then continue
round their track until they reach any of the farm parking
spaces, where they can place the animal card in their
farm pen. There are six shaded parking spaces for the
farm and market, to ensure that players land on a 'farm'
and a 'market' square each time round. Continue playing
until all the animals are sold. When the last animal set is
bought, play stops immediately and the players count up
how many animals they each have (the total number of
animals, not animal cards). Remember to count the
animals in the Land Rovers. The player with the most
animals is the winner. As the Land Rovers are larger than
the track squares, it is important that all players mark
their positions on the board accurately, placing the front
of the vehicle on the square they have reached.

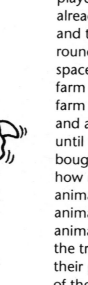

TEACHER'S ROLE

As the game develops, the players should all keep a record of their scores to practise addition and number bonds. The children could write out number sentences to show their running totals, and this could be extended to a subtraction number line to show how the total number of animals in the market decreases during the game. An inventory for each farm can be written out, e.g. blue farm: 3 sheep, 4 pigs, 10 chicks = 17 animals altogether. Ask questions to develop number bonds at the end of the game. For example: if the blue farm wanted 20 sheep, how many more would it need to buy? The children could draw a block graph, using a colour key to record the animals purchased by each farm (as shown on the left).

This game offers various other opportunities for recording data, as shown on the photocopiable record sheets.

Sheet 64 is a pictorial record of the animal groups, which can be coloured in as the game progresses. The totals can be calculated and written in at the end.

The dotted triangle on sheet 65 is another, more diagrammatic method of recording the animal groups: the number lines can be coloured in as each corresponding set of animals is sold. The overall total for each farm and their respective positions can also be recorded.

For all of the above, additional animal cards could be made to extend the number values involved in the game, and new record sheets could be designed to cater for this.

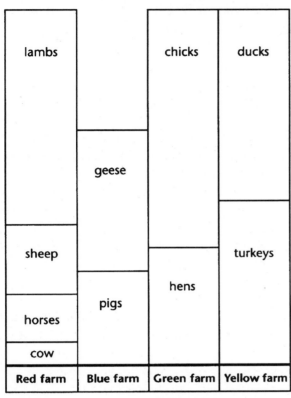

The blocks representing each animal set should be proportional to the number of animals within that set.

EXTENSION

☆ Practising simple multiplication using money (N: 4b; M: B)
☆ Using decimal fractions with money (N: 2c; RTN: C)
☆ Using calculators for calculating with real data (N: 1d, 3e; RTN: B)

This game can be adapted to expand upon the theme of buying and selling. Instead of simply exchanging the sets of animals for a £1 coin each time, a price could be set for each animal. So: if horses were to cost £50 each, the two-horse set would be worth a total of £100. Decimal numbers and the decimal notation of money could be introduced if the price of a goose, for example, were set at £6.50 each. The set of six geese would then cost £39.00. The prices of animals should, of course, be set according to the ability of the children. The record sheet on page 66 provides a template for this alternative, whereby the teacher can fill in the prices before the game and the children can then calculate how much they have spent on each animal group, and their total expenditure. Which player spent the most? Which set of animals was the most expensive? Which single animal was the most expensive? Which was the cheapest? The children could estimate the cost of each animal set, and then use a calculator to work out the exact total before entering it on the record sheet.

HOW TO PLAY TO MARKET, TO MARKET

For 2 to 4 players

YOU NEED: a bag of 1 to 10 number cards, a game board, a set of 1 to 10 animal cards, a Land Rover for each player, nine £1 coins for each player, a dice and shaker.

❶ Place all of the animals in the market square and the Land Rovers on the 'start' square for each farm.

❷ Take nine £1 coins and place them on the circles next to each farm.

❸ Take turns to throw the dice and move your Land Rover the number of spaces thrown around the track.

❹ When you reach any of the market parking spaces (the shaded squares), you can draw a number from the bag. You can now buy the matching set of animals.

So: if you draw a 3, you can buy the 3 sheep.

❺ Return the card to the bag. Take a £1 coin from your farm and place it in the market square. Put the animal card in your Land Rover.

❻ Continue around the track. When your Land Rover reaches any of the farm parking spaces (the shaded squares), place the animal card in the farm pen.

❼ Continue playing in this way until the last set of animals has been sold.

❽ Add up the total number of animals on your cards. The player with the highest total is the winner.

☆ REMEMBER!

If the set of animals matching your card has already been sold, wait until your next turn to draw another card. You must collect a set of animals before moving on.

ANIMAL CARDS

Colour, cut out, fold, glue and hold.

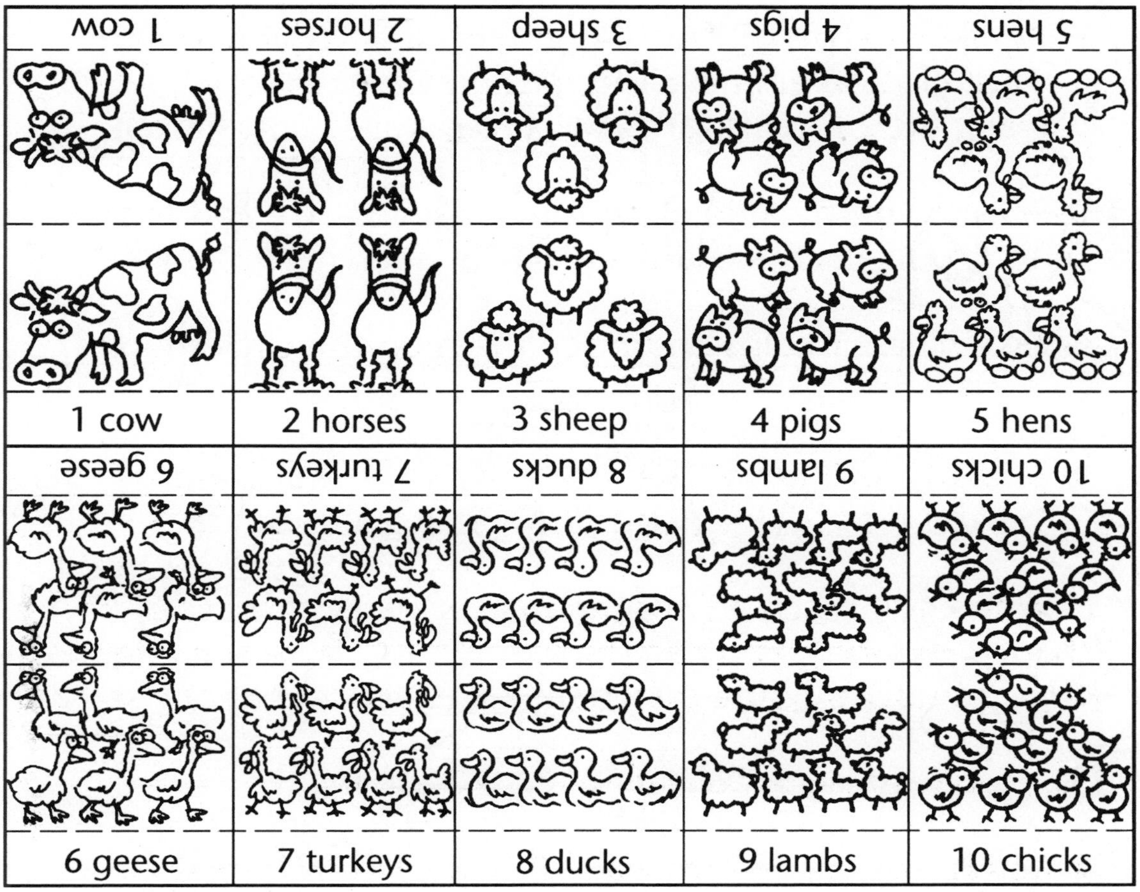

1 cow	2 horses	3 sheep	4 pigs	5 hens
1 cow	2 horses	3 sheep	4 pigs	5 hens
6 geese	7 turkeys	8 ducks	9 lambs	10 chicks
6 geese	7 turkeys	8 ducks	9 lambs	10 chicks

NUMBER TILES

Cut out and put in a bag.

| 1 | 2 | 3 | 4 | 5 |
| 6 | 7 | 8 | 9 | 10 |

RECORD SHEET 1 FOR TO MARKET, TO MARKET

Use your coloured pencil to draw a ring around
each group of animals as you buy them.

Now work out the total for each farm.

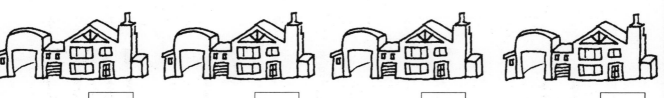

red farm
total

blue farm
total

green farm
total

yellow farm
total

RECORD SHEET 2 FOR TO MARKET, TO MARKET

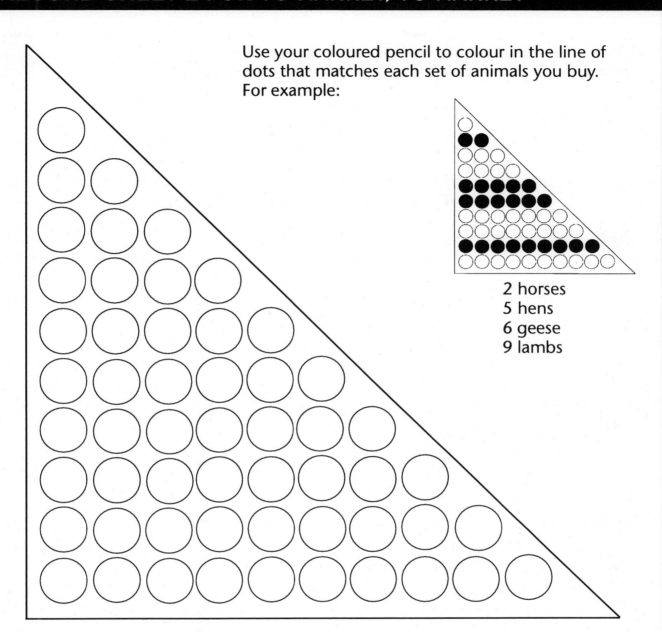

Use your coloured pencil to colour in the line of dots that matches each set of animals you buy. For example:

2 horses
5 hens
6 geese
9 lambs

Now work out the total for each farm and write in who came 1st, 2nd, 3rd and 4th.		total	position
	blue farm	animals	
	green farm	animals	
	yellow farm	animals	
	red farm	animals	

TO MARKET, TO MARKET EXTENSION SHEET

Write in the colour of your farm. Calculate how much you spent on each set of animals. How much did you spend altogether?

	farm bought

animal	price each	total
1 cow		
2 horses		
3 sheep		
4 pigs		
5 hens		
6 geese		
7 turkeys		
8 ducks		
9 lambs		
10 chicks		

grand total

PHOTOCOPIABLE PAGES

1 to 100 number cards sheet 69, bingo cards sheet 70, 'How to play' sheet 68.

FOR CONSTRUCTION

Card, scissors, adhesive (optional).

FOR PLAYING

Pencils or counters, 'How to play' sheet, a bag containing a set of 1 to 100 cards, a bingo card for each player.

BINGO 100

TEACHING CONTENT

☆ Using numbers from 1 to 100 (N: 2b; RTN: B)

☆ Recording and recognising numbers including odd and even (N: 1e; RTN: B)

PREPARATION

Assembling the game: Cut up photocopiable sheet 69 to make the 1 to 100 number cards and place them inside a bag. Cut up photocopiable sheet 70 to make individual bingo cards. If the players cross out the numbers on their cards as they are drawn, it will be cheaper to photocopy the bingo cards on to paper (they will only be used once). If the players cover their numbers with counters or coins, it may be better to use card.

Introducing the game: Many children may be familiar with the concept of bingo from competitions in the national newspapers. Much of the bingo caller's jargon ('two fat ladies – 88', 'two little ducks, quack, quack – 22', 'legs eleven' and so on) is associated with the visual appearance of numbers and can be amusing as well as instructive.

HOW TO PLAY

This is a game for two or more players. Each of the players or teams needs a hollow square bingo card. The teacher, or an appointed child, then draws number cards from the bag, calling out the numbers each time and allowing the players to check their cards and cross off the number if it is there. The first player to cross off three numbers in a line is the winner. It is important that the 'caller' keeps a record of the numbers that have been drawn in order to check that the winner has indeed won. A copy of photocopiable sheet 69 can be used for this purpose.

TEACHER'S ROLE

This game can provide a good indication of problems that children are experiencing in making and recognising numbers. To develop children's understanding of number, it may be helpful if the teacher expands on simply calling out the number. For example, calling 'Eighty-six, eight tens six ones' will help the children to understand how our numbers are constructed. When a child claims to be the winner, check the numbers using the bingo card sheet. In this way, the children can begin to appreciate the need to keep records and check data. The bingo squares are made up of either odd or even numbers. Does the winner have an 'odd' or 'even' square? What type of square do the other players have? What are the numbers on their squares? As extra practice in using a calculator, ask the children to add up all of the numbers on their squares and to write the total in the blank square in the middle of the card. Who has the highest total? For purposes of extending or varying the activity, we have included blank number cards to be filled in by the teacher.

GAME VARIATIONS

Instead of specifying a line of three numbers to win, the players could try for four – the four corner squares or the four central squares on each side of the card.

HOW TO PLAY BINGO 100

For 2 or more players

YOU NEED: a set of 1 to 100 number cards, a bag, a hollow square bingo card and a pencil for each player.

❶ Choose who will be the bingo caller.

❷ Put all of the number cards into the bag and give each player a bingo card and a pencil.

❸ The caller draws number cards from the bag and calls out their value, allowing the players to check their bingo cards each time before drawing another number.

If the number is on your card, you can cross it off.

❹ Continue playing. The first player to cross off three numbers in a line, either horizontally or vertically, is the winner.

☆ NOW!

Add up all of the numbers on your bingo card and write the total in the empty square at the centre of your board. Use a calculator to do this if necessary.

Who has the highest total?

1 TO 100 NUMBER CARDS
Cut up this sheet to make individual number cards.

1	2	3	4	5	6	7	8	9
10	11	12	13	14	15	16	17	18
19	20	21	22	23	24	25	26	27
28	29	30	31	32	33	34	35	36
37	38	39	40	41	42	43	44	45
46	47	48	49	50	51	52	53	54
55	56	57	58	59	60	61	62	63
64	65	66	67	68	69	70	71	72
73	74	75	76	77	78	79	80	81
82	83	84	85	86	87	88	89	90
91	92	93	94	95	96	97	98	99
100								

BINGO GAMEBOARDS

6	100	52	5	65	29	8	66	30
76		88	77		89	78		90
40	64	28	41	53	17	42	54	18
7	67	31	10	68	32	9	69	33
79		91	80		92	81		93
43	55	19	44	56	20	45	57	21
12	70	34	11	71	35	14	72	36
82		94	83		95	84		96
46	58	22	47	59	23	48	60	24
13	73	37	16	74	38	15	75	39
85		97	86		98	87		99
49	61	25	50	62	26	51	63	27

BULL'S EYE

TEACHING CONTENT

★ Knowing number names and understanding number values from 1 to 20 (N: 2a, 2b; RTN: A)

★ Understanding addition and subtraction with numbers up to 20 (N: 3b, 4a; AS: B)

PREPARATION

Assembling the game: Copy, or mount, photocopiable sheet 33 on to card. It can then be cut up to make individual number cards. A bag is then needed to hold the cards so that the players cannot see which ones they are drawing. You can use either the digit or dot number cards. Cut up photocopiable sheet 73 to make individual record strips for the game.

Introducing the game: Explain that the bull's eye is the highest score on a target. Number games using targets can be used in the classroom for basic addition activities. Familiarity with adding numbers 1 to 10 is also needed.

HOW TO PLAY

This is a game for two to four players. Before distributing a number strip to each player, the teacher fills in the target number in the space on the right and explains that the players' aim is to make up this total by adding together the number cards they draw from the bag. This number will vary according to the ability of the children. The players take turns to draw a number card from the bag. Each player must then decide whether to keep the card and place it on her strip, or return it to the bag hoping for a better number next round. If a player keeps a number card and goes bust, or keeps too many small numbers to make the target number even if she draws a 10 for her last card, she is out of the game. Players keep track of their scores in the smaller squares below their number lines. The first player to collect number cards that add up to make the 'bull's eye' number is the winner, but play continues until every player has reached the target number or has gone bust.

TEACHER'S ROLE

During the game, help the children to keep track of their scores and ask questions to help them decide which cards they should keep. How many more do you need? Do you want a number card higher than 5/lower than 5? Encourage them to be exact and develop strategies for playing the game successfully. The smaller boxes below the number line are there so that the players can keep a running total. At the end of the game, the players can write out the values of the cards in their sequence to make a number sentence. Working backwards along the number line in the smaller boxes may help them to do this.

GAME VARIATIONS

The game can be adapted for use with higher numbers by using the 1 to 100 number cards on photocopiable sheet 69. If appropriate, extra squares could be added at the beginning of the bull's eye strip. The game can be simplified by using a 1 to 6 dice and setting the target number accordingly, or the objective could be to make the highest/lowest number.

HOW TO PLAY BULL'S EYE

For 2 to 4 players

YOU NEED: a bag of 1 to 10 number cards, a bull's eye record strip for each player, pencils.

❶ The teacher fills in the target number for each player in the space on the right of the number strip.

❷ The players now take turns to draw cards from the bag and place them on the squares on their number strip. The aim is to collect cards that add up to make the bull's eye number.

Each turn, you must decide whether to keep the card or return it to the bag and wait for your next turn.

❸ Write down your new total each time you take a card in the small squares below the number line.

❹ The first player to collect cards that add up to make the target number is the winner. Continue playing to find out who finishes 2nd, 3rd and 4th.

❺ Colour in the box on your strip to show your finishing position.

☆ REMEMBER!

If your score adds up to more than the target number, you have gone bust.

If you have one space left on your number strip but you need a number higher than 10 to make the target number, you cannot win and are out of the game.

RECORD SHEET FOR BULL'S EYE

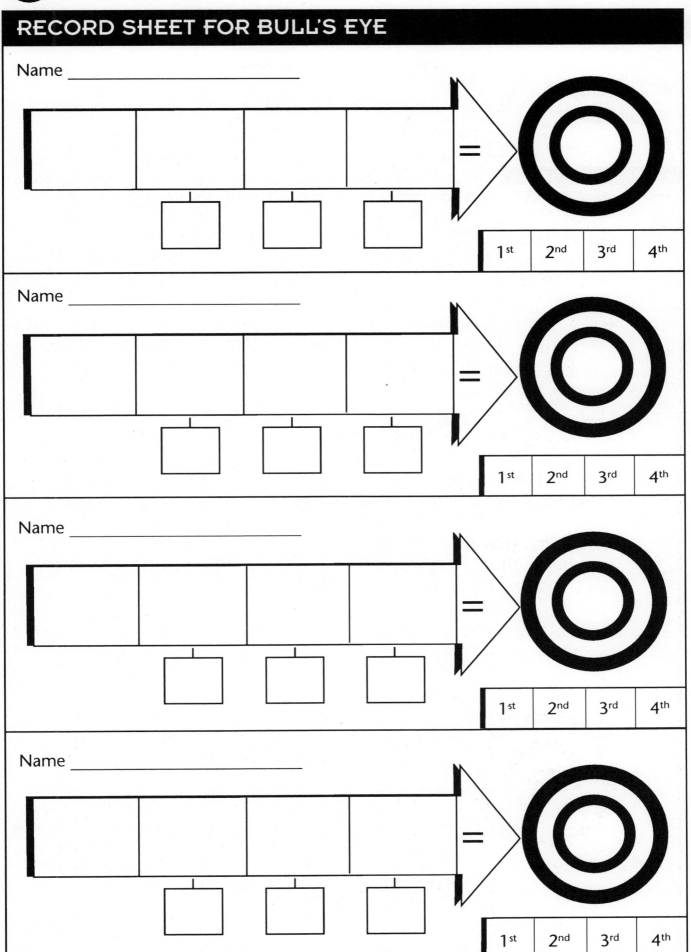

Name _____

| 1st | 2nd | 3rd | 4th |

Name _____

| 1st | 2nd | 3rd | 4th |

Name _____

| 1st | 2nd | 3rd | 4th |

Name _____

| 1st | 2nd | 3rd | 4th |

PHOTOCOPIABLE PAGES
*Baseboard sheet 77,
roundabout base and sides
sheets 78 and 79, 'How to play'
sheet 76.*

FOR CONSTRUCTION
*Card, scissors, glue, a brass
paper fastener, coloured crayons
or pens.*

FOR PLAYING
*Toy coins (a 1p, 2p, 5p, 10p,
20p and 50p for each player),
'How to play' sheet, the
roundabout, a dice and shaker.*

FAIR'S FARE

TEACHING CONTENT

☆ Recognising coin values: 1p, 2p, 5p, 10p, 20p and 50p (N: 4a; M: A, B)

PREPARATION

Assembling the game: Photocopy sheet 77 twice and stick the two halves of the baseboard together. Colour each of the sections of the baseboard in a different colour. Photocopy the base and sides of the roundabout (sheets 78 and 79) once, then assemble the roundabout as indicated on page 75. The roundabout can be coloured in before assembly to make it look more attractive. A hole needs to be pierced through the centre of the baseboard and base of the roundabout – a brass paper fastener can then be used to secure the roundabout to the baseboard. Make sure that the roundabout turns freely before playing the game.

Introducing the game: Ask the children if any of them have been to a fair or taken a ride on a roundabout in a park playground. Look at the roundabout in this context in order to help them understand the principle of the game: how the faces of the roundabout are likely to land on a different section of the baseboard in each turn.

HOW TO PLAY

This game is best played by six or three players. Give each player a set of toy coins up to 50p (a 1p, 2p, 5p, 10p, 20p and 50p). Each player then chooses a coloured section of the baseboard (or if there are three players, each player chooses two sections). The players can only use their nominated sections during the game. Each player takes a coin and places it on her section of the baseboard (or a coin on each of her two sections if there are three players). Players take turns to roll the dice and turn the roundabout in a clockwise direction according to the number thrown. So, if a 2 is thrown the roundabout is turned so that each of the faces moves round two sections on the baseboard. Now look at the values shown on the sides of the roundabout. If the value on a side of the roundabout matches the coin on the section on which it has landed, then the player who placed the coin can remove it from the board and place it inside the roundabout itself. Coins remain in place on the baseboard until they are matched, and can then be replaced with another coin before play continues. The first player to use all of her six coins is the winner.

TEACHER'S ROLE

This game will help children in matching coins to their written values. Make sure when playing that the roundabout is moved correctly. For example, if a 3 is thrown the roundabout is turned so that each face moves through three of the coloured sections on the baseboard. Look at the values on the faces of the roundabout. Ask the children to say out loud the value of the face that has landed on their section of the board. Is it the same as their coin? It is important that the players match the value to the coin correctly in order to play the game successfully. Ask the children to say the name of the coin they place on the board each time, to develop coin recognition. When a player has 'won', look at how the other players are doing. Final positions can be determined by the number of coins each player has left. This will provide further opportunities for counting and coin recognition. How many coins does each player have left? What is their total value? Look at the coins the winner has used. How many coins has she used? What is their total value? Use 1p coins for counting and exchange purposes if this is helpful to the children.

GAME VARIATIONS

• For a simplified version of the game, restrict all of the players to using only one coin value in each round. There can be a winner of each round or a point can be scored for each round, and players can add up their totals after six rounds.

• The game could be adapted to develop shape recognition by making six different shape cards for the players and replacing the coin values on the sides of the roundabout with these shapes.

CONSTRUCTION DIAGRAM FOR ROUNDABOUT

❶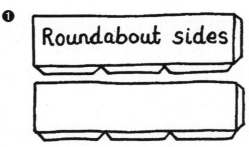

Cut out sections.

Roundabout base

❷ Fold and glue sides, then position on top of base and glue.

 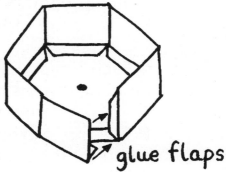

glue flaps

❸ Fasten to baseboard, leaving the roundabout free to turn.

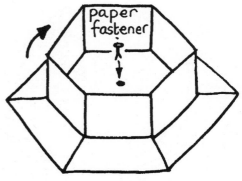

paper fastener

HOW TO PLAY FAIR'S FARE

For 2 to 6 players

YOU NEED: the roundabout, a dice and shaker, a 1p, 2p, 5p, 10p, 20p and 50p coin for each player.

❶ Make sure each player has a complete set of six coins.

❷ At the beginning of the game each player chooses a coloured section of the baseboard on which to play, then places one of her coins on this section. No more than one coin can be placed on a section.

❸ Players take turns to roll the dice and turn the roundabout the same number of spaces in a clockwise direction.

So: if a 2 is thrown, the roundabout is turned so that each face moves round two sections of the baseboard.

❹ Look at the coin value on the side of the roundabout that has landed on your section of the board. If it matches your coin, you can remove your coin and put it in the centre of the roundabout.

❺ Each time your coin is matched, place another coin on your section of the board and continue playing.

❻ The first player to place all six of her coins in the centre of the roundabout is the winner.

ROUNDABOUT BASEBOARD

Mount two sheets on card and stick the two pieces together.

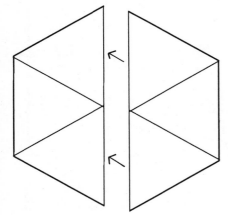

Colour in each section with a different colour, for example:

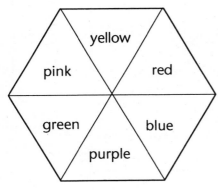

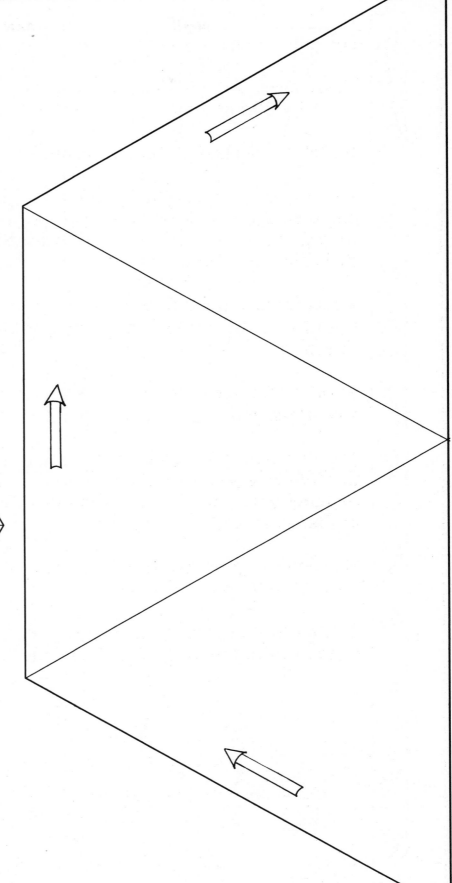

ROUNDABOUT SIDES Colour, cut out, fold and glue. See page 75 for construction.

BASE FOR ROUNDABOUT

Cut out and attach to sides of roundabout as indicated below.
See page 75 for construction.

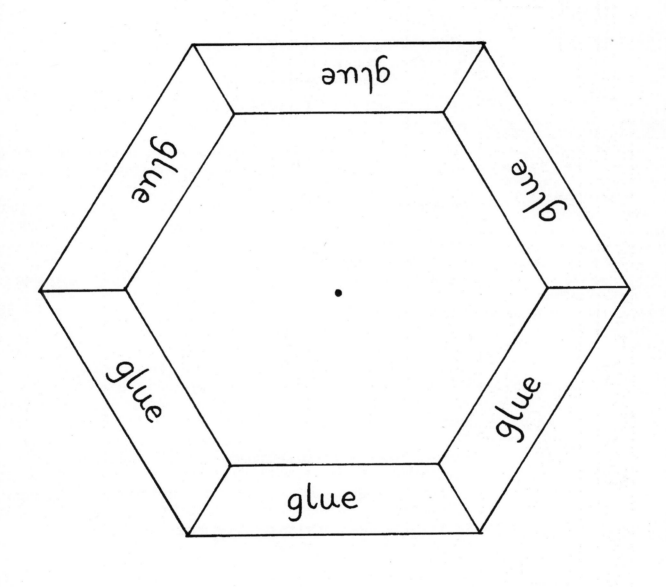

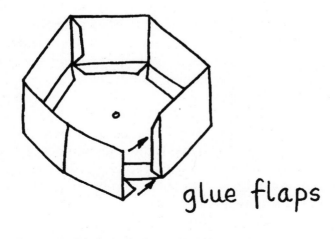

glue flaps

SOLDIERS ON PARADE

TEACHING CONTENT

☆ Developing concepts of sets by counting collections and checking the total (N: 1a, 2a, b; PS: A)

☆ Using addition and subtraction with numbers to 12 (N: 3b, 3c; AS: A, B)

PREPARATION

Assembling the game: Make the spinners and ranks of soldiers as indicated on photocopiable sheets 83 and 84. One full set of soldiers is needed per player. The soldiers can be coloured in to make them more attractive.

Introducing the game: The activity game 'Ten tall soldiers' (page 15) can be used to prepare the children for this activity. Have any of the children seen military parades, either in real life or on the television? How do the soldiers line up? In one line or in rows? How often do soldiers have to perform parade drill? Perhaps the children could hold their own parade.

HOW TO PLAY

This is a game for two or more players. Each player has a set of soldier figures showing the values 1 to 6, which he places in the middle at the beginning of each game. The teacher, or one of the players, then spins the spinner to determine how many soldiers need to be collected. The players then take turns to throw a dice, and take that number of soldiers from the middle. So: if they throw a 3, they take a rank of three soldiers. They can, however, choose to pass if they do not wish to collect that number of soldiers. The skill is in deciding which numbers to take and which to leave. No player can collect the same rank value more than once (if he already has a rank of two soldiers and throws a 2, that throw does not score). The winner is the first player to get the exact number of soldiers in his line-up. If a player collects more soldiers than the target number, he is out of the game.

TEACHER'S ROLE

Explain that the target number changes each game and is determined by the spinner. During the game, ask questions to draw attention to the number of soldiers each player has: How many ranks of soldiers do you have? Which ranks do you have? How many soldiers does that make altogether? How many do you need to make the target number? Which ranks can you use to make up this number? At the end of the game, you can work backwards from the target number to develop subtraction skills. What is the total number of soldiers? If we take away the rank of 4 soldiers, how many are left? These can be written out as number sentences to demonstrate number bonds. Copies of the ranks of soldiers can be placed alongside addition and subtraction number sentences to make a visual display.

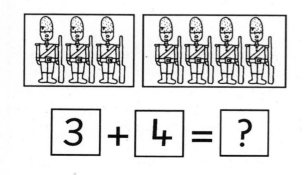

GAME VARIATIONS

• A simpler version of this game is to see who is the first to collect a full set of soldiers, i.e. one rank of all values from 1 to 6. The players take turns to throw the dice and collect the equivalent rank from the middle. If they already have that rank, their throw does not score. The first player to get all the soldier ranks from 1 to 6 wins.

• Alternatively, the players could take turns to throw the dice and collect the rank of soldiers matching their throws each time. If all of the ranks for that number are gone, the throw does not score. Play ends when there are no soldier ranks left. The winner is the player with the highest total of soldiers.

• In another version, players could be allocated certain number values so that one player only collects ranks of 2, another only ranks of 4 and so on. The first player to collect all of the ranks of his allocated value from the middle is the winner.

EXTENSION

★ Counting collections of objects, checking the total (N: 2a, 2b; PS: A)
★ Understanding addition and subtraction for numbers 1 to 20
   (N: 3b, 3c; AS: A, B)
★ Sorting and classifying objects (N: 5a; IH: A)

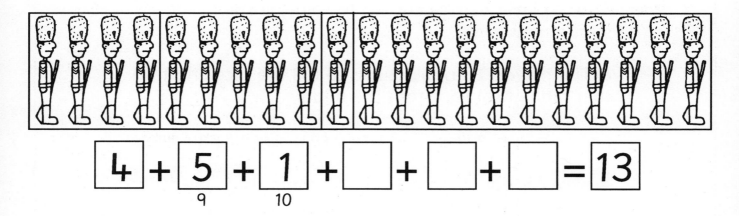

This game can be extended by using a spinner with the values 13 to 20 to determine the number of soldiers to be collected. Again, all of the ranks of soldiers are placed in the middle and collected according to the numbers thrown on the dice. Give each player a copy of record sheet 85, so that they can keep a visual record of their progress. Make sure they understand that they have to draw a vertical line between the soldiers on the record sheet to indicate the size of the rank of soldiers they collect each turn (as shown in the illustration above). Some children may need help with this and at first may try to draw round the soldiers one at a time, effectively counting in ones rather than adding the numbers together. Encourage them to write down their scores each round in the number line on the record sheet, and to keep track of their total as the game progresses. Ask questions during the game: What is your score now? How many more soldiers do you need to make the exact total? Can the children tell from their record sheet how many turns it took them to make the exact total?

   (NB For this version of the game, two sets of soldiers will be needed per player.)

HOW TO PLAY SOLDIERS ON PARADE

For 2 or more players

YOU NEED: a complete 1 to 6 set of soldiers for each player, the number spinner, a dice and shaker.

❶ Place all of the ranks of soldiers in the middle.

❷ Choose one player to spin the spinner. The number thrown gives the target number for this game.

So: if the spinner lands on 8, all of the players must try to make a line-up of 8 soldiers for that game.

A new player can be chosen to spin the spinner to start a new game.

❸ The players then take turns to roll the dice and take that rank of soldiers from the middle.

So: if a player rolls a 5, he can take a rank of 5 soldiers.

A player is not allowed to collect more than one rank of each value.

So: If a player rolls a 2 and he already has a '2' rank of soldiers, that throw does not score.

❹ The first player to collect the target number of soldiers in his line-up is the winner.

PLAYING PIECES   Colour, cut out, fold, glue and hold.

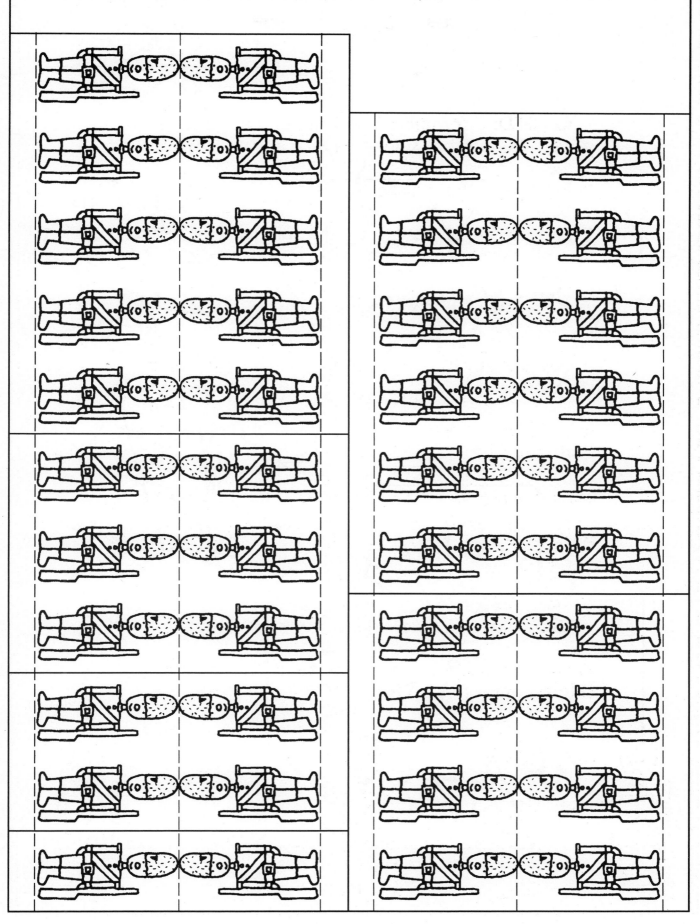

SPINNERS

Cut out and push a pencil through the centre.

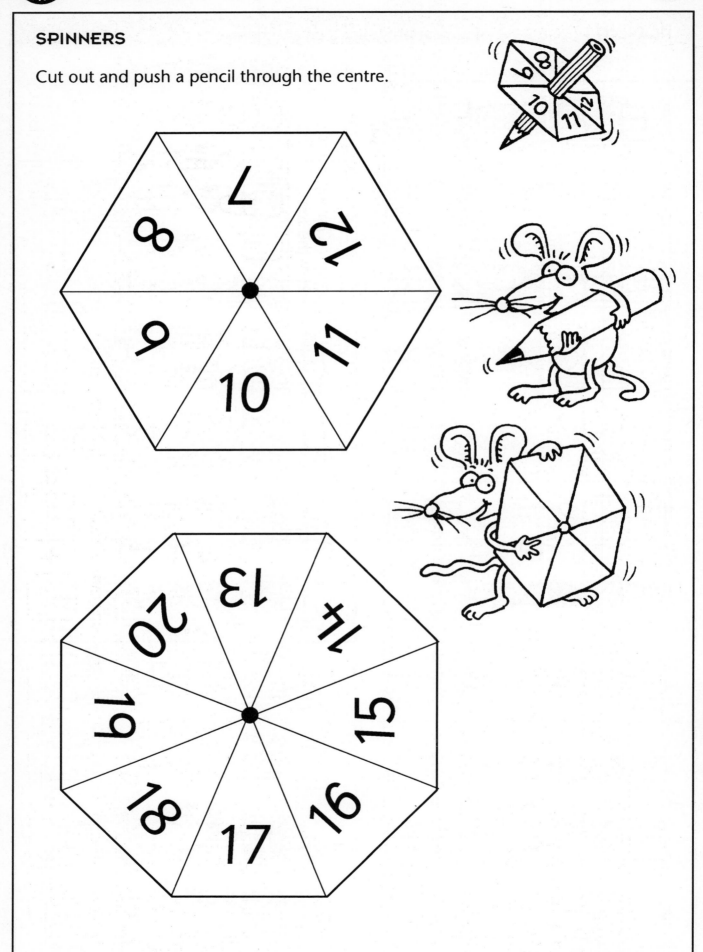

RECORD SHEET FOR SOLDIERS ON PARADE

Write the number of soldiers needed for the line-up in the box.
Cross out the extra soldiers at the end of the strip.

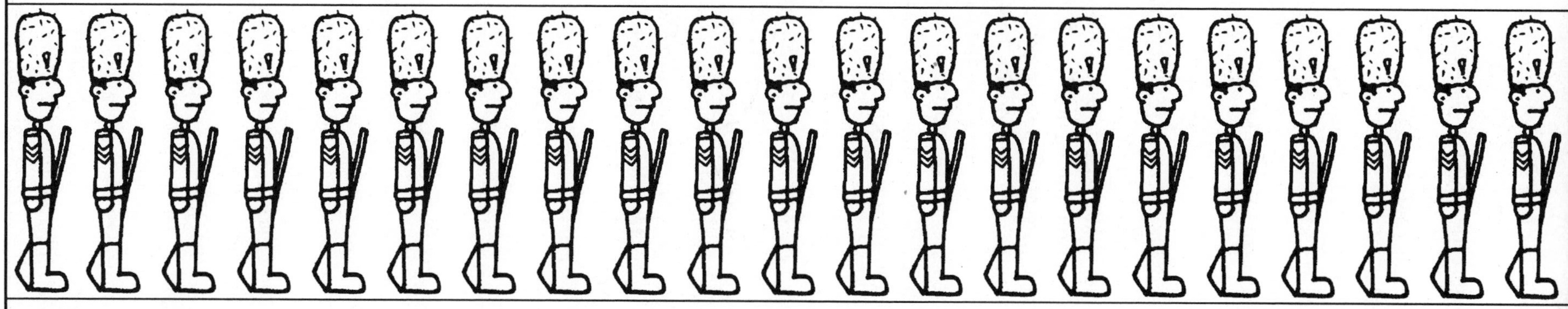

Name _____

Draw a vertical line on your strip to show each rank of soldiers you pick up.

☐ + ☐ + ☐ + ☐ + ☐ + ☐ = ☐

was the winner.

Write the number of soldiers needed for the line-up in the box.
Cross out the extra soldiers at the end of the strip.

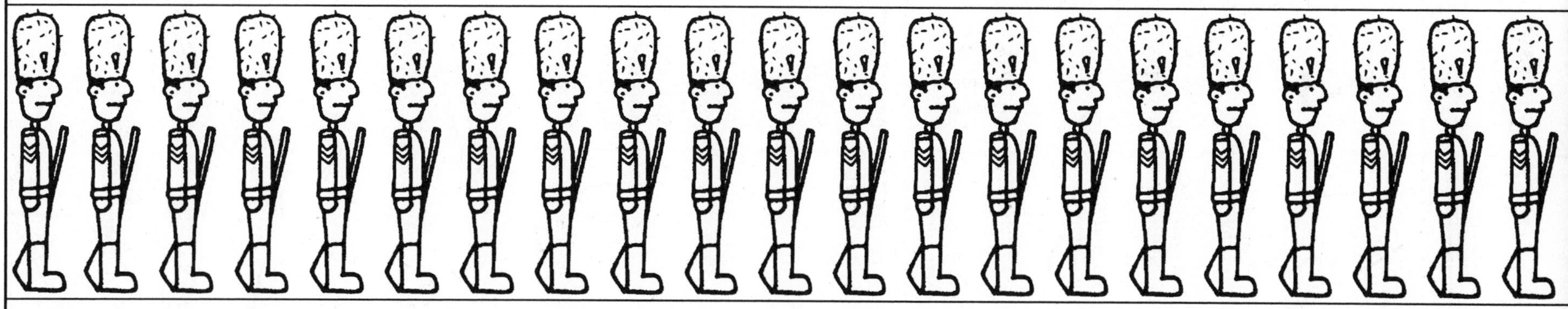

Name _____

Draw a vertical line on your strip to show each rank of soldiers you pick up.

☐ + ☐ + ☐ + ☐ + ☐ + ☐ = ☐

was the winner.

85

PENNY PURSE

TEACHING CONTENT

★ Counting orally from 1 to 10 knowing the number names (N: 1a; RTN: A)
★ Recognising and using 1p and 10p coins (N: 1a; M: A)
★ Counting and collecting (N: 2a; RTN: A)
★ Exploring addition and subtraction patterns to 10 using money (N: 2b, 3a, b; AS: A)
★ Beginning to understand that one object (a 10p coin) can represent a set of similar but lower-valued objects (N: 2a, 4b; M: B)

PREPARATION

Assembling the game: A coin purse needs to be made for each player (photocopiable page 90). The children can colour in their purses before assembly to make them more attractive. A 10p insert card is then placed inside. To play the game, a dice showing only the values 1 to 3 is needed. This can be done by covering 4, 5 and 6 with sticky labels and drawing on dots 1 to 3 (facing their matching values, so 1 is opposite 1 and so on).
Introducing the game: Children could count the money in their own purses or in 'purses' prepared by the teacher to develop coin recognition. How many of each type of coin are there? What is the total amount for each coin type? Can they say how much there is altogether?

HOW TO PLAY

This is a game for two or more players. The aim of the game is to fill the purse with 1p coins to make up the value of the 10p coin in the centre. The players take turns to throw the dice and collect the number thrown in 1p coins from the coin bag. They then place the coins on the 1p spaces in their purse. In the final stage, they must throw the exact number required to fill their purse in order to collect the silver 10p coin. So: if they have two spaces left to fill and they throw a three, that throw does not score. The first player to fill his purse is the winner. If you do not wish the game to end at this point, continue playing to decide on the other places or until every player has finished.

WHAT YOU NEED

PHOTOCOPIABLE SHEETS
Coin purse template sheet 90, insert cards sheets 88 and 89, 'How to play' sheet 88.

FOR CONSTRUCTION
Scissors, card, adhesive, coloured crayons, sticky labels.

FOR PLAYING
A coin purse and insert card for each player, 'How to play' sheet, a bag of 1p coins (ten per player), one 10p coin per player, a restricted 1-3 dice and a shaker.

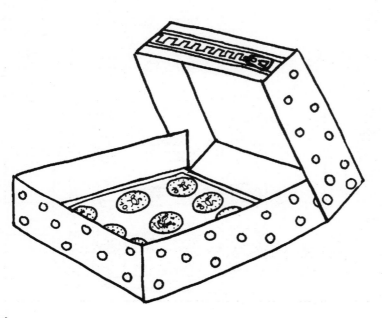

TEACHER'S ROLE

It is not immediately obvious to young children how and why money serves as our means of exchange in everyday life. This simple game can be used to help develop children's understanding of the concept of money, demonstrating how 10 x 1p becomes 1 x 10p. Throughout the game, ask questions to stimulate the children's mathematical thinking. How much money do the players have in their purses? How many more coins do they need to fill their purses? Make sure that the children count the spaces and do not guess. When everyone has completed the game, ask the children to count the coins in their purses. Some will say they have ten, counting only the 1p coins; but the more astute may answer 20, or more than ten, if they are unsure how to count 10p and 1p coins together. Go through an adding sequence starting from 10p, adding 1p to the total each time, as a demonstration. This can be done in reverse (working down from 20p, 10p or an even lower total) to demonstrate subtraction.

EXTENSION

☆ Counting collections to 20, 50 and 100 checking the total (N: 2a; M: B)
☆ Read, write and order numbers to 100 (N: 2b; RTN: B)
☆ Recognising and using coins (N: 1a; M: A)
☆ Exploring addition and subtraction patterns to 20, 50 and 100 using money (N: 3b, 3c, 4a; AS: B)
☆ Exploring patterns in 2×, 5× and 10× tables (N: 3b; MD: B)

This game can also be adapted for use with 2p and 20p coins, 5p and 50p coins and 10p and £1 coins, using the insert cards on photocopiable sheet 89 and an adapted 'How to play' panel. In addition, a bag of the relevant coins for each game will need to be provided. In this way, children can be encouraged to use progressively larger numbers in a practical context – and, at the same time, to develop their understanding of money and how one object can represent a set of similar objects of lower value. As preparation for this, the children could play a game with 1p and 2p coins, throwing an ordinary dice and collecting that number of 2p coins. They can then exchange their 2p coins for the equivalent value in 1p coins, reinforcing the relationship between the two and providing a practical example of the 2× table. The children can make a coin pyramid to demonstrate this (as shown below). This can be extended to demonstrate the 5× and 10× tables, using larger coin values. To give an added dimension to the game, one face of the restricted dice could be left blank – when this is thrown, the player scores 0.

Throughout the game, stimulate children's mathematical thinking with questions similar to those given on the previous page, but adapted for the money values being used.

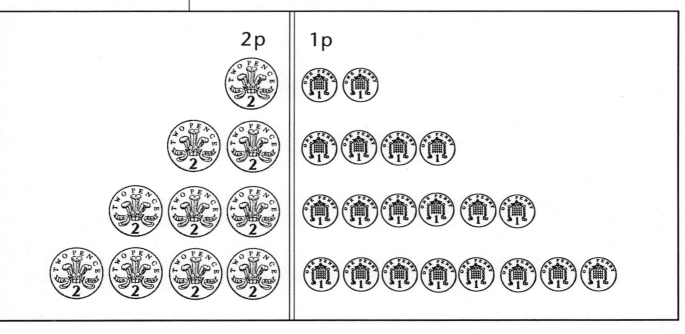

HOW TO PLAY PENNY PURSE

For 2 or more players

YOU NEED: a coin purse and coin insert for each player, ten 1p coins and one 10p coin per player, a dice and shaker.

❶ Place the coins in the middle.

❷ Take turns to throw the dice and collect the number thrown in 1p coins.

If you throw a 3, you collect three 1p coins.

❸ Place the 1p coins on the 1p spaces inside your purse.

❹ Continue playing. The first player to cover all ten of the 1p spaces in his purse and collect a silver 10p to place in the middle of them is the winner.

☆ REMEMBER!

To finish, you must throw the exact number you need.

If you have nine 1p coins in your purse, you must throw a 1 to win.

Any other number does not score.

PENNY PURSE INSERT CARD

Cut out to make insert card.

PENNY PURSE
INSERT CARDS

Cut up to make insert cards.

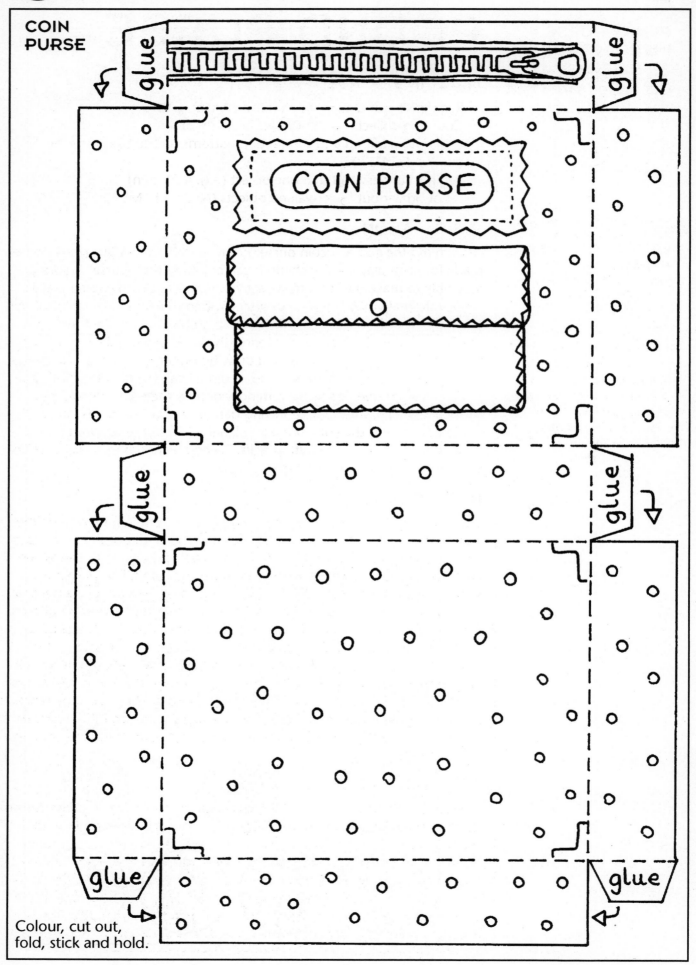

COIN
PURSE

COIN PURSE

glue glue glue glue

Colour, cut out,
fold, stick and hold.

POUND PURSE

TEACHING CONTENT

★ Recognising and using coins (N: 1a; M: A)
★ Counting collections to 100 (N: 2a; RTN: B)
★ Exploring addition and subtraction patterns to 100 using money
  (N: 3b, 4a; AS: B)
★ Begin to understand that one object (e.g. a £1 coin) can represent a
  set of similar but lower-valued objects (N: 2a, 4b; M: B)

PREPARATION

Assembling the game: A coin purse (photocopiable sheet 90) needs to be made for each player – the children can colour in their purses before assembly to make them more attractive. A £1 insert card is then placed inside (alternative £1 insert cards are provided to extend the range of the game). A dice showing the coin values 1p, 2p, 5p, 10p, 20p and 50p is needed. This can be made by covering the faces of a building block or standard dice with sticky labels and drawing on the coin values. Toy coins in all values should be provided and a coin till can be used to store these – this will also serve as a visual reminder of how the coins are ordered.
Introducing the game: Simple sorting games and question-answer sessions involving the coins we use will help to develop children's confidence and coin recognition skills. Playing 'Penny purse' (page 86) is a good introduction to this game.

HOW TO PLAY

This is a game for two or more players. The aim of the game is to fill the purse, making up the value of the £1 coin in the centre of the insert card with coins of smaller denomination. The players take turns to throw the coin dice and collect the value thrown from the coin till. If there is a space free for this type of coin on their insert card, they can place the coin in their purse. If there is no space available for that denomination of coin, they must return it to the till. The first player to cover all of the coin spaces on her insert card is the winner and collects the £1 coin.

There are three £1 insert cards provided, all showing different ways in which the £1 total can be made up using the coins of lower value. At first it might be best if all the players use the same card insert; but once they are more confident with the game, they could each use a different insert to add variety and to demonstrate that there are many ways to make up the £1 total.

TEACHER'S ROLE

It might be helpful to look at the coins featured on the insert cards. Some duplication of coin values is inevitable, but looking at how these work together (e.g. 2p + 2p + 1p + 5p = 10p) can help to reinforce number bonds. As the game is being played, ask the players how much money they have collected. How much more do they need to win? Which coins make up this amount? If the alternative insert cards are used, look at the various ways of making up the £1 total. The children could be invited to find their own ways of making the £1 total and devise their own card inserts. This could form the basis for display work.

WHAT YOU NEED

PHOTOCOPIABLE SHEETS
Coin purse template sheet 90, insert cards sheet 93, 'How to play' sheet 92.
FOR CONSTRUCTION
Scissors, card, adhesive, coloured crayons, sticky labels.
FOR PLAYING
A coin purse and insert card for each player, 'How to play' sheet, a coin till containing many 1p, 2p, 5p, 10p, 20p and 50p coins and one £1 coin, a coin dice and a shaker.

GAMES

HOW TO PLAY POUND PURSE

For 2 or more players

YOU NEED: a coin box and £1 insert card for each player, a till containing a large selection of 1p, 2p, 5p, 10p, 20p and 50p coins and a £1 coin, a coin dice.

❶ Take turns to throw the dice. Look at the coin value thrown each turn.

If there is a space available for that coin on the insert card inside your purse, you can take the coin from the till and place it in your purse.

If there is no space available the throw does not score.

❷ Continue playing. The first player to cover all of the coin spaces in her purse so as to make the total of £1 is the winner. She can collect the £1 coin and place it in the middle of her purse.

POUND PURSE
INSERT CARDS

Cut up to make insert cards.

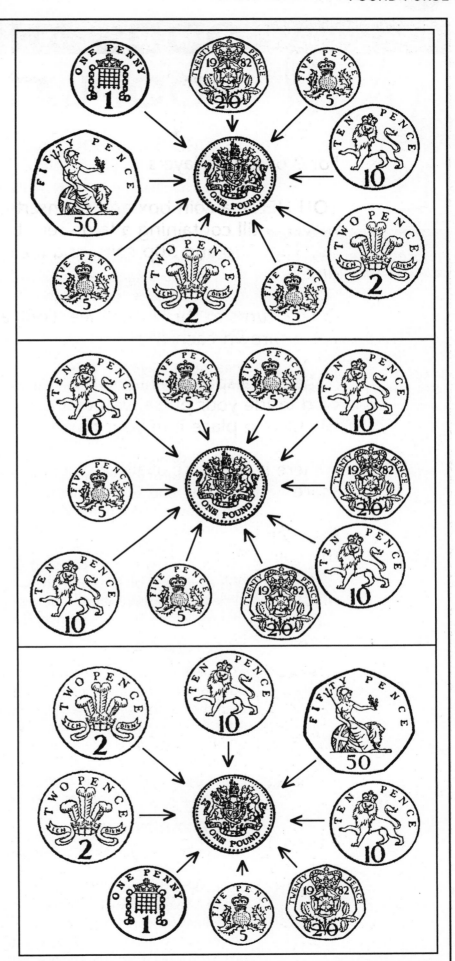

WHAT YOU NEED

PHOTOCOPIABLE SHEETS
Game sheet 96, 'How to play' sheet 95.

FOR CONSTRUCTION
A building block or dice, sticky labels, a pen.

FOR PLAYING
An odds and evens dice, a game board, 'How to play' sheet, a different coloured crayon for each player.

ODDS AND EVENS HOOPLA

TEACHING CONTENT

☆ Counting orally and knowing the number names, including odd and even numbers (N: 2a; RTN: A, PS: B)
☆ Recording in a variety of ways (N: 1e; IH: A)

PREPARATION

Assembling the game: An odds and evens dice is needed (cover the six faces of a building block or standard dice with sticky labels, and make three of the faces 'odd' and three 'even'). As the game sheet will be written on, it is more economical to photocopy it on to paper.

Introducing the game: Many children will have seen hoopla stalls at the fair and will be familiar with the idea that putting a ring round an item means that they have 'collected' that item. Children need to understand the concept of odd and even numbers before playing this game.

HOW TO PLAY

This is a game for two or more players. Each of the players needs a different coloured crayon. Only one game sheet is needed. The players then take turns to roll the dice; but before they do so, they must nominate 'odd' or 'even'. If they nominate 'even' and roll 'even', they can choose an even number on the game sheet and circle it using their coloured crayon. If they nominate 'odd' and roll 'odd', they can choose an odd number on the game sheet and circle it using their coloured crayon. Otherwise, they cannot draw a circle. Continue playing until all of the numbers on the game sheet have been circled. The player who has circled the most numbers is the winner. Alternatively, you could specify that the winner is the player whose numbers have the highest total.

TEACHER'S ROLE

Ask questions during the game to make sure that the children recognise odd and even numbers correctly. What number is one more, or one less, than the number they have chosen? Are these numbers odd or even? After the game, look more closely at the characteristics of odd and even numbers. Can you divide an even number by 2? What about an odd number? Try adding two even numbers together – is the total odd or even? Try adding two odd numbers – is the total odd or even? What happens if you add together an odd number and an even number?

GAME VARIATION

This could be played as an actual game of hoopla for two players. Make skittles numbered 1 to 10 out of card tubes. Rings can be made by slicing a plastic bottle (horizontally) into circular sections, five rings for each player. Make sure any rough edges are smoothed away. One player nominates to score on odd numbers only and the other on even. If a player scores on a skittle of the wrong type, or on a skittle that is already taken, he loses that turn. The first player to 'hoop' all his numbers wins.

HOW TO PLAY ODDS AND EVENS HOOPLA

For 2 or more players

YOU NEED: the hoopla game sheet, an odds and evens dice, a different coloured crayon for each player.

❶ Take turns to roll the dice – but before you throw, guess whether you are going to score 'odd' or 'even'.

If you say 'even' and the dice rolls 'even', you can circle an even number on the game sheet using your coloured crayon.

If you say 'odd' and the dice rolls 'odd', you can circle an odd number.

Choose any number you like that has not been taken already.

If you do not guess correctly, you cannot circle a number.

❷ Continue playing until all of the numbers have been circled.

❸ The player who has circled the most numbers is the winner.

ODDS AND EVENS HOOPLA GAME SHEET

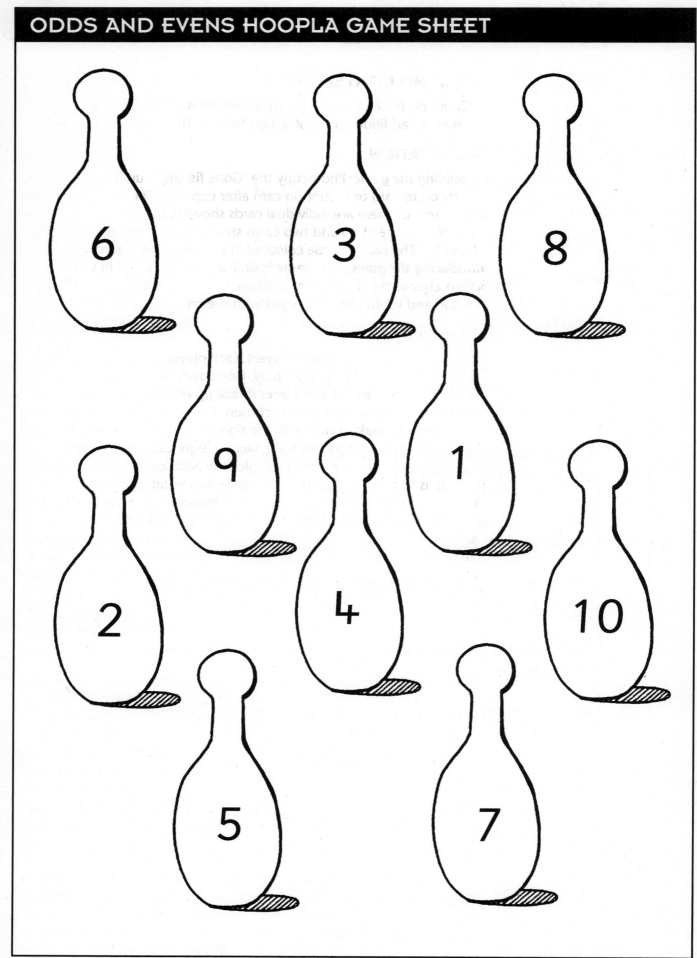

WHAT YOU NEED

PHOTOCOPIABLE SHEETS
*Fish number cards sheet 99,
'How to play' sheet 98, record
sheet 100.*
FOR CONSTRUCTION
Card, scissors, crayons.
FOR PLAYING
*A set of fish number cards, 'How
to play' sheet, pencils, score
record sheet.*

GONE FISHING

TEACHING CONTENT

☆ Counting orally and knowing the number names (N: 1a; RTN: A)
☆ Knowing addition and subtraction facts to 30 (N: 3c; AS: B)

PREPARATION

Assembling the game: Photocopy the 'Gone fishing' number cards
directly on to card or mount on card after copying. They need then to be
cut out so that there are individual cards showing the values 0 to 10, one
card with a value of 20 and two cards showing the mathematical signs
'+' and '−'. The cards can be coloured in to make them more attractive.
Introducing the game: This game is similar to a 'lucky dip' in that the
players choose the numbers at random. It may be useful to run through
addition and subtraction strategies with the children before the game.

HOW TO PLAY

This is a game for two or more players. Each player needs a record sheet.
All of the cards are placed separately, face down, in the middle. The first
player picks up one card and places it face up on the table. She continues
picking cards until a 'sign' card is chosen. She must then choose two of
the numbers to make a sum with the sign card – the aim being to make
the highest number possible. If she picks a 'sign' card before selecting at
least three numbers, she must then pick the additional number card(s).
The idea is that the players should choose two numbers from at least
three, thus deciding which are the best numbers to use with the number
sign. If two sign cards are drawn, one must be chosen and the other
returned immediately to the middle. The player then writes down the
sum she has made on her record sheet, and all of the cards are returned
to the centre for the next player to take a turn. (It may be best to 'shuffle'
the cards before each turn to make sure that the choice is random.) The
player who makes the highest number wins that round and scores a point.
Play five rounds. The winner is the player with the most points at the end.

TEACHER'S ROLE

This game provides an opportunity to practise addition and subtraction
skills. Encourage the children to try out the various alternatives their
numbers offer and, in this way, to develop strategies for making the
highest number. If you are adding numbers together, which two make
the highest total? If you are subtracting, which two make the highest
total? Can you make rules which tell you what to do when adding, or
subtracting, numbers if you want to make the highest total possible? Of
course, any player lucky enough to pick the 20 card will have an
advantage, but the same principles of addition and subtraction still apply.

GAME VARIATION

To make the game more interesting for the children, it can be adapted to
be played as a traditional 'fishing' game. Attach paper-clips to each of
the playing cards and then make 'fishing rods' from dowelling and a
piece of string with a small magnet tied to the end. The cards can be
placed in a box before the children fish for their numbers.

HOW TO PLAY GONE FISHING

For 2 or more players

YOU NEED: a set of fish number cards, pencils, a record sheet for each player.

❶ Place all the cards separately, face down, on the table.

❷ The first player picks a card and turns it face up.

❸ That player continues to pick cards and lay them out, face up, until one of the sign cards (+ or –) is picked.

❹ She must then look at the numbers and the 'sign' she has picked and select TWO of the numbers to make a sum. The aim is to make the HIGHEST number possible.

So: if you pick a 4, 8, 2, 5 and the '+' card, you would choose 8 + 5 = 13

Or: If you pick 4, 8, 2, 5 and the '–' card, you would choose 8 - 2 = 6

❺ When a player has made a sum, return all the cards to the centre, shuffle them and the next player can take a turn.

❻ Continue playing until every player has taken a turn. The player with the highest total wins a point.

❼ Play five rounds. The winner is the player with the most points at the end.

☆ REMEMBER!

You must choose from at least THREE numbers. If you pick a 'sign' card before you have three numbers, you may pick other cards.

If you pick two 'sign' cards, choose one and return the other to the centre.

GAMES

FISH NUMBER CARDS
Colour and cut out to make individual cards.

1

2

3

4

5

6

7

8

9

10

0

+

−

20

RECORD SHEET FOR GONE FISHING

Write a number sentence for each of your turns.

For example: =

Score a point if your score is the highest.

Points

Round 1

   = 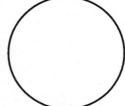   _____

Round 2

    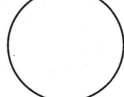   _____

Round 3

       _____

Round 4

    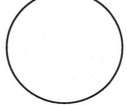   _____

Round 5

    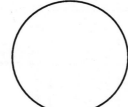   _____

Total points:

Where did you finish?
Circle your position.   1st   2nd   3rd   4th

HIGH OR LOW?

TEACHING CONTENT

☆ Developing a variety of methods for adding and subtracting two-digit numbers (N: 3d; AS: B)

☆ Choosing the appropriate operation to solve a problem (N: 4c; AS: C)

☆ Using a calculator (N: 1d, 4c; AS: B, C)

PREPARATION

Assembling the game: Photocopy page 69 directly on to card (or mount on to card after copying). Cut up the sheet to make the 1 to 100 number cards and place them in a bag. One copy of photocopiable sheet 103 is needed for each pair of players.

Introducing the game: Although this appears a fairly simple game, the children need to understand the importance of developing a strategy. In trying for highest and lowest numbers, they will need to make choices based on their opponent's existing totals. Make sure they understand how the record sheet works.

HOW TO PLAY

This is a game for two players. Each player in turn draws two numbers from the bag of 1 to 100 number cards. The player can choose whether to add the numbers together or subtract one from the other, and may use a calculator. When he has decided what to do, he enters the numbers, the chosen operation symbol and the total on the record sheet (as shown in the example in the margin). Each player has five turns, and the cards are returned to the bag after each turn. The winner is the player who is able to get both the highest and the lowest total. If no one wins, the game is a draw: play again.

TEACHER'S ROLE

To a large extent, the teacher's contribution to this game depends on the ability of the children. Ask questions during the game to prompt the children's mathematical strategies: What number will you make if you add these two numbers? What if you subtract them? Which total is the highest? Which is the lowest? Which number do you want to keep? Why? It can be useful to look at each player's record sheet at the end of the game. Which rounds did they score/lose points? If they had chosen differently, would they have won that round? Can they understand why?

GAME VARIATION

A hundreds version can be played by adding another column of boxes to each side of the record sheet. Instead of using the 1 to 100 number cards, use the 1 to 10 cards on photocopiable page 33, altering the 10 to 0. Players draw single digits from the bag and make them into hundreds numbers by writing them down in strict order – 3 followed by 5 followed by 1 becomes 351 (three hundred and fifty-one). Return those cards to the bag before drawing for the second number each turn. Children should write the numbers in pencil, since the second number they draw may be larger than the first, and if they decide to subtract, they will need to put the larger number on top.

WHAT YOU NEED

PHOTOCOPIABLE SHEETS
Record sheet 103, 1 to 100 number cards 69, 'How to play' sheet 102.

FOR CONSTRUCTION
Card, adhesive, scissors.

FOR PLAYING
Record sheet, bag of 1 to 100 number cards, 'How to play' sheet, 2 pencils, a red and a blue pen.

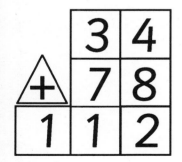

HOW TO PLAY HIGH OR LOW?

For 2 players

YOU NEED: the record sheet, a bag of 1 to 100 number cards, 2 pencils, a red and a blue pen.

The aim of the game is to be the player who makes both the highest and the lowest number.

❶ Choose who will be Player 1 and Player 2.

❷ Take it in turns to draw two numbers from the bag of 1 to 100 number cards. Choose whether you want to add these numbers or subtract one from the other. Write down your sum on the record sheet.

If you choose 56 and 22, you could make:

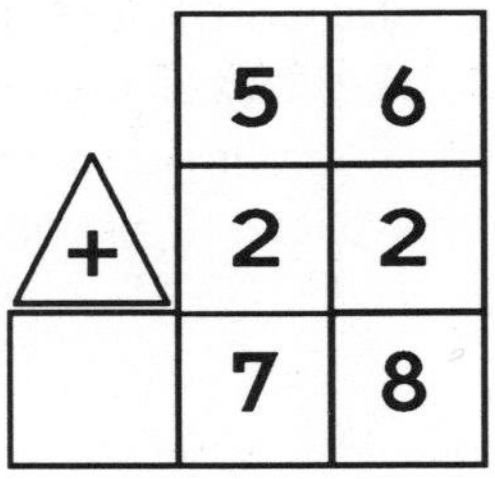

	5	6
+	2	2
	7	8

or

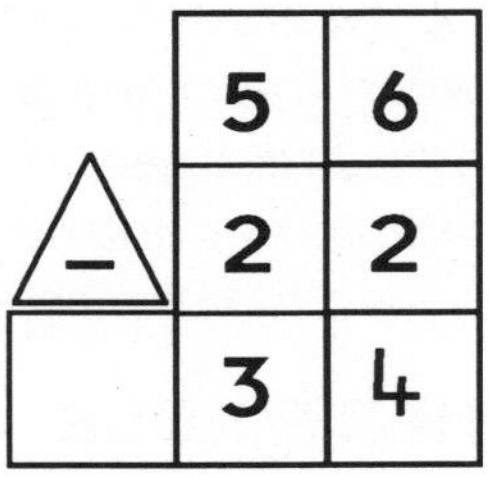

	5	6
−	2	2
	3	4

❸ After each turn, return the cards to the bag and shake the bag before the next player draws two numbers.

❹ Take five turns each and record your scores each round.

❺ Now look at your scores. Circle your highest score in blue and your lowest in red.

❻ The player who has made both the highest and the lowest score is the winner. If neither player has won, you must play the game again.

PHOTOCOPIABLE GAMES

ROUND THE BLOCK

TEACHING CONTENT

☆ Developing suitable methods of computation for addition, subtraction, multiplication and division (N: 3c, 4c; AS: B, MD: B)
☆ Checking answers by different methods and gaining a feel for the appropriate size of an answer (N: 4d)
☆ Using a calculator (N: 3e, 4c, d; MD: B)

PREPARATION

Assembling the game: Photocopy sheets 69, 106 and 107 on to card. Cut up the calculator cards sheet to make individual cards and the 1 to 100 sheet to make individual number cards. The number cards should be placed in a bag. The game can be varied for any range of numbers you want the children to practise. You can also adapt the game sheet for operations other than addition.

Introducing the game: Ensure that children are aware of the range of numbers and mathematical operations you have chosen to practise.

HOW TO PLAY

This is a game for two to four players. Unlike the pattern of most other games, here all players move around the board together. The counter, which is used to mark all players' positions, is put on the Start/Finish square and the set of calculator cards is placed in the middle of the board. One of the players picks two number cards from the bag and places one on each square of the first building. This produces a sum for the children to calculate. The counter is moved on to the first building to indicate that this is the sum the players are working on, and the timer is then set for an agreed time. The players work individually to calculate and write the answer on their paper. When the time is up, they use the calculator to check the answer. Players who get the answer wrong take a calculator card from the centre. The number cards are put back into the bag, the counter is moved to the next building and the process is then repeated. This continues until the players have been right 'round the block' and are back to the Start/Finish square. The player with the fewest calculator cards at the end is the winner.

TEACHER'S ROLE

This game can be adapted for a range of numbers and for all the various operations. The teacher needs to establish the needs of the particular group playing and adjust the playing sheet and number bag accordingly. She will also need to set a time limit for each turn and make sure the children understand that they should take turns to pick the number cards out of the bag and set the timer. During the game, observation will reveal those children who have grasped (or are beginning to grasp) the addition process and can show their 'workings' on paper (although if the numbers drawn out of the bag are easy, the children may well be able to work the answers out mentally). Are they able to deal with place value in two-digit numbers? Do they add the 'ones' before adding the 'tens'? After the game, discuss with them their methods of calculation. Can they use known facts to find new results?

WHAT YOU NEED

PHOTOCOPIABLE SHEETS
Game sheet 107, calculator cards sheet 106, 1 to 100 tiles sheet 69, 'How to play' sheet 105.

FOR CONSTRUCTION
Card, scissors, adhesive, clear adhesive plastic, coloured pen or pencils.

FOR PLAYING
Game sheet, a set of calculator cards (8 per player), 'How to play' sheet, a bag of 1 to 100 tiles, a timer, a calculator, a counter, paper and pencil for each player.

HOW TO PLAY ROUND THE BLOCK

For 2 to 4 players

YOU NEED: a game sheet, a set of calculator cards (8 per player), a bag of 1 to 100 number cards, a timer, a calculator, a counter, and paper and a pencil for each player.

❶ Place the counter on the Start/Finish square and the set of calculator cards in the middle of the board.

❷ Choose one of the players to pick two tiles from the bag and place one on each square of the first building. This makes a sum, for example:

$$23$$
$$+ \; 52$$

❸ Move the counter on to the first building to show that this is the sum that all players must work out.

❹ Set the timer for the time limit given by the teacher. Each player then works individually to calculate the answer and write it on down on paper.

❺ When the time is up, use the calculator to check the answer. Players who get the answer wrong must take a calculator card from the centre.

❻ Put the number cards back into the bag and move the counter to the next building.

❼ Continue playing in this way, taking turns to draw number cards, until the players have been right 'round the block' and are back to the Start/Finish square.

❽ The player with the fewest calculator cards at the end is the winner.

CALCULATOR CARDS   Cut out. There are enough for two players.

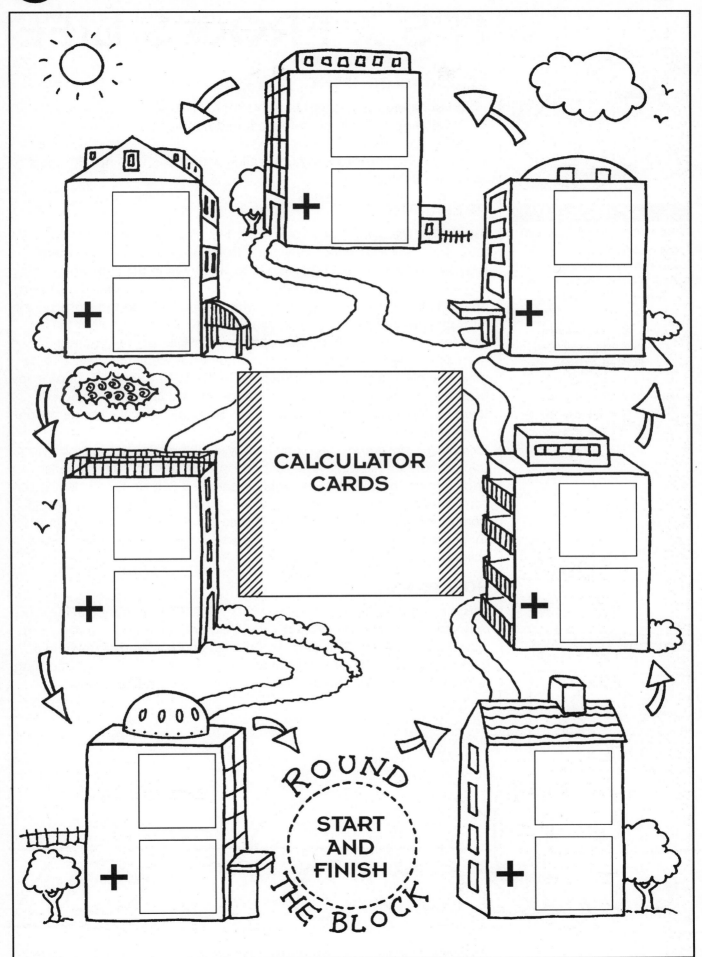

IT'S A FROG'S LIFE

TEACHING CONTENT

★ Investigating the concept of 0 (N: 2b; RTN: A)

★ Developing a variety of methods for adding and subtracting (N: 3d; AS: B)

★ Introducing the idea of a number line with plus and minus numbers (N: 2c; RTN: B)

PREPARATION

Assembling the game: Photocopy sheet 113 twice on to thin card (or mount on card after photocopying). Cut the strips out and glue them together to form one long playing strip, as shown in the illustration on page 109. Note that you will only need one of the strips with the 0 (zero) on it. Mark the stone on the far left with a minus (–) and the stone on the far right with a plus (+). You may wish to write 'Finish' or colour in the last stone on the right-hand side of the strip. Make up the required number of frog playing pieces as shown on photocopiable sheet 134. To make the playing cards on photocopiable sheets 111 and 112, photocopy both sheets directly on to card (or mount on card afterwards) and cut them up. Colour in the components as you prefer, to make the game look more attractive.

Introducing the game: This game links well with a science topic on living things and their habitats. It focuses on issues of survival – in particular finding food and shelter, and avoiding enemies. Explain the underlying concepts to the children: the frog moves forward (+) for food, retreats (–) from foes or enemies who might eat them, and stays put when it finds shelter or cover (+ 0 or – 0). Introduce any unfamiliar vocabulary to the children.

HOW TO PLAY

This is a game for two or more players. If more than four are playing, you may want to extend the playing strip in either direction. The players start with their frogs on 0. The cards are shuffled and placed face down in a pile. In turn, each player takes the top card and moves her frog according to the instructions on the card (as shown in the illustration below).

WHAT YOU NEED

PHOTOCOPIABLE SHEETS
Game strip sheet 113, game cards sheets 111 and 112, frog playing pieces sheet 142 and 'How to play' sheet 110.

FOR CONSTRUCTION
Card, scissors, adhesive, coloured pens or pencils.

FOR PLAYING
Stones playing strip, a frog playing piece for each player, 'How to play' sheet, a set of playing cards.

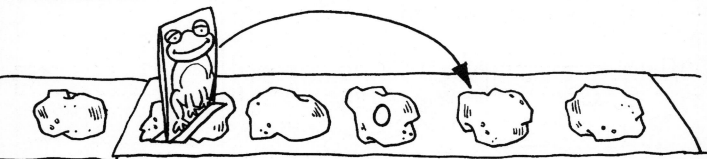

If you pick the beetle 'food' card you move forward 3 spaces.

Finding food enables a player to move forward, encountering an enemy means she must move back; finding suitable cover means she stays where she is. The used cards are then placed in a pile to one side. If a score takes a player beyond the stone on the far left then she places her frog on the last square on the left. If she then picks up a minus ('You meet a foe') card, she just stays put. She can only move again with a plus ('You find food') card. The first player to put her frog on the stone on the far right by drawing the card with the exact number is the winner. If the pack of cards is used up before the game ends, reshuffle the 'used' pile and resume the game until someone wins.

TEACHER'S ROLE

This game is an investigation of 0. Do not be tempted to use just one name for 0. Throughout, draw the players' attention to 'zero' as a central place on the line of stones (or as a place on a scale such as a ruler or thermometer) and to 'nought' as a quantity (or absence of it) when adding and subtracting. The 'You find cover' cards have either + 0 or − 0 on them, in order to develop children's understanding that the concept of 0 as 'no value' is the same whether you are adding it or subtracting it. Note those children who, when they pick a cover card, actually try to move their frogs and those who understand straight away that they must stay put. During the game, question the children about their frog's position: How far is it to the finish (i.e. the stone on the far right)? What number do you need? What sign will you need on the card? How near to zero are you? What sign is needed on a number card to get you back to zero? The stones on the strip do not have numbers, other than 0, as this would necessitate having − 1, − 2 and so on. However, if you wish to introduce negative numbers, you can write these in.

GAME VARIATIONS

• Introduce an additional rule which says that only one frog can be on a space at a time. If a frog lands on an already occupied stone, that frog sends the first frog back to zero. Ask the children: When is this a penalty (when a frog is to the right of 0) and when is it a reward (when a frog is to the left of 0)?
• Make the stone strip longer and add further food and foe cards with higher number values, for example 7, 8, 9, 10.

CONSTRUCTION OF GAME BOARD

Photocopy game board sheet 113 twice and cut up the pages to make individual strips. Stick five strips together with one of the 0 strips at the centre and two of the blank strips on either side, as shown in the diagram below.

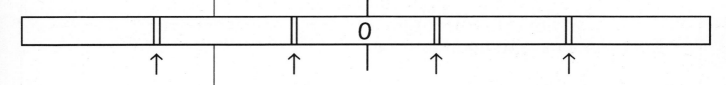

Use the tabs at the end of each strip to stick the strips together.

HOW TO PLAY IT'S A FROG'S LIFE

For 2 or more players

YOU NEED: a stones playing strip, a frog playing piece for each player, a set of playing cards.

❶ Put the frogs on the stone marked 0.

❷ Shuffle the cards and place them face down in a pile.

❸ Take it in turns to take the top card and move your frog according to what the card says.

You find food. (+)	Move to the right the number of spaces shown.
You meet a foe. (−)	Move to the left the number of spaces shown.
You find cover. (+ 0 or − 0)	Stay where you are.

❹ After your move, place the card in a pile to one side.

❺ The first player to place her frog on the stone on the far right is the winner. The exact number to reach this stone must be drawn.

☆ REMEMBER!

If you are on the stone on the far left and you pick a 'You meet a foe' card, you cannot move. You must wait until your next turn and move only when you draw a 'You find food' card.

FROG'S LIFE CARDS

Cut up this sheet to make individual cards.

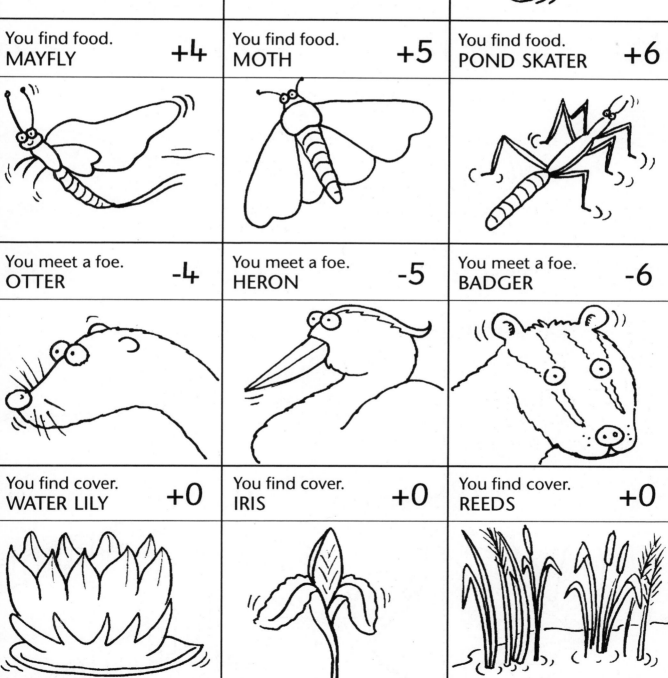

You find food. SLUG +1	You find food. SNAIL +2	You find food. BEETLE +3
You find food. MAYFLY +4	You find food. MOTH +5	You find food. POND SKATER +6
You meet a foe. OTTER -4	You meet a foe. HERON -5	You meet a foe. BADGER -6
You find cover. WATER LILY +0	You find cover. IRIS +0	You find cover. REEDS +0

FROG'S LIFE CARDS
Cut up this sheet to make individual cards.

You meet a foe. FOX -1	You meet a foe. KESTREL -2	You meet a foe. CROW -3

You meet a foe. GRASS SNAKE -1	You meet a foe. CAT -2	You meet a foe. PIKE -3

You find food. BUTTERFLY +1	You find food. FLY +2	You find food. DRAGONFLY NYMPH +3

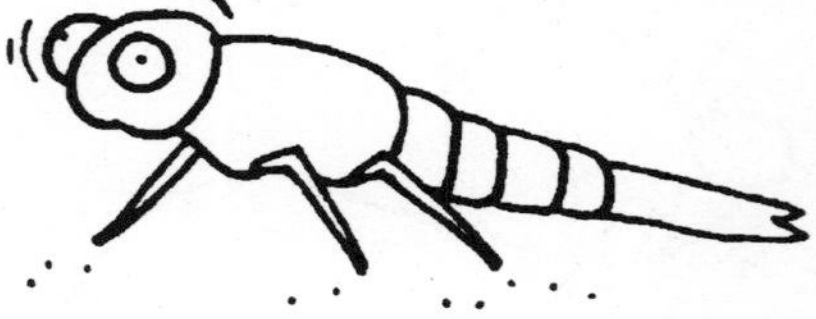

You find cover. WATERCRESS -0	You find cover. PONDWEED -0	You find cover. MOSS -0

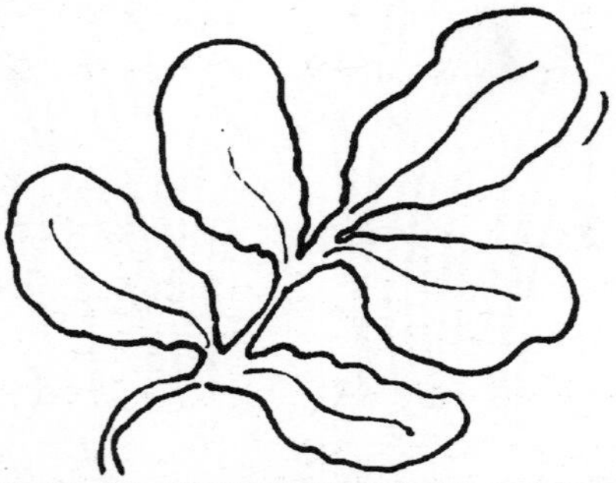

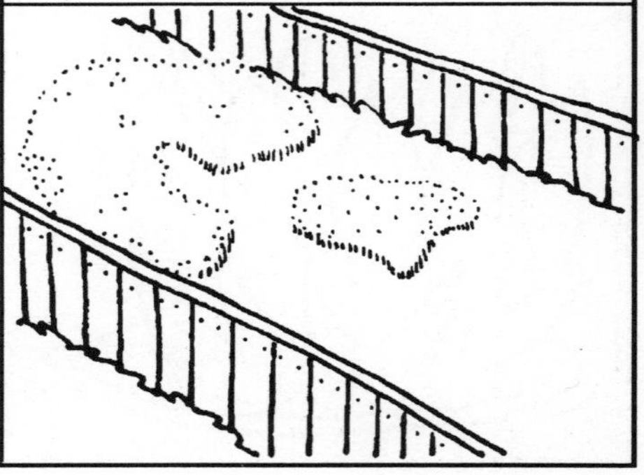

GAMES

GAME BOARD

Cut this sheet into three strips. See page 109 for construction instructions.

 x2

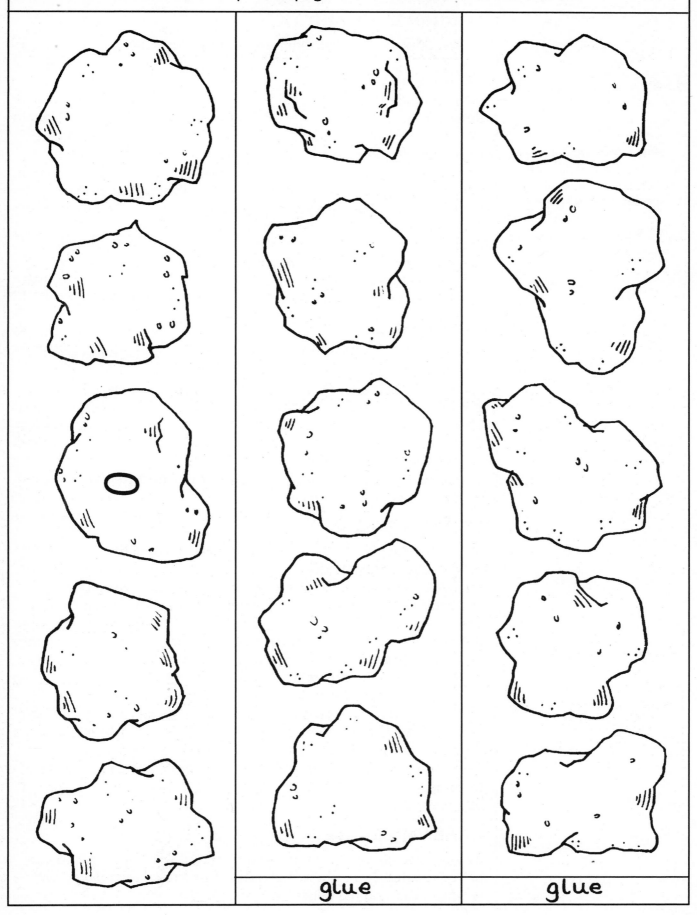

glue   glue

WHAT YOU NEED

PHOTOCOPIABLE PAGES
Cake pieces sheets 116 and 117, 'How to play' sheet 115.

FOR CONSTRUCTION
A building block or dice, sticky labels, crayons or coloured pencils, card, adhesive (optional).

FOR PLAYING
Cake pieces, 'How to play' sheet, a fraction dice.

PIECE OF CAKE

TEACHING CONTENT

☆ Recognising and using simple fractions (N: 2c; RTN: B)

PREPARATION

Assembling the game: There are six cakes – three divided into halves and three into quarters. Photocopy cake pieces sheets 1 and 2, then colour in the cakes using three different colours so that there are two complete cakes in each colour (one divided into halves and one into quarters). A fraction dice is also needed. This can be made by covering the faces of a building block or dice with sticky labels and colouring opposite faces in the same colour. You then write the fractions $1/2$ and $1/4$ on the labels, so that there is a $1/2$ and a $1/4$ for each colour.

Introducing the game: Slicing cake is something practically all children will have seen, and is one of the simplest ways to demonstrate basic fractions. Before playing the game, use the cake pieces to make sure that the children understand how many halves or quarters make a whole.

HOW TO PLAY

This is a game for two or three players. Before starting, decide whether the players need to make one or two whole cakes to win. Each player chooses one of the cake colours and must then try to collect a whole cake (or cakes) in his nominated colour. Place all of the 'cake' cards face up in the centre. Players take turns to throw the fraction dice. If you throw a $1/2$ in your colour, you can collect a 'half' cake card; if you throw a $1/4$, you can collect a 'quarter' cake card. If you do not throw your colour, you do not collect a card. The first player to make a whole cake (or two whole cakes) is the winner.

TEACHER'S ROLE

As the children play the game, watch to make sure that they understand how the numerical fraction on the dice represents one of the pieces of cake. Ask questions while the game is in progress to develop their understanding of fractions: How many quarters/halves do you have? How many pieces do you need to make a whole cake? How do you write this as a fraction? Discuss how to read the fractions: $1/2$ means one part of two parts, $1/4$ means one part of four parts. How many quarters make a half? Is three-quarters more than a half? Once the children are comfortable with halves and quarters, progress to smaller fractions if you feel this is suitable. Ask questions: What would happen if I cut a half into two slices? Would the pieces be bigger or smaller than quarters? If I cut a quarter into two pieces, how many of these pieces would make half a cake? How many would make a whole cake? How many would make three-quarters of a cake? Use the cake pieces to investigate this. Look at other fractions.

GAME VARIATIONS

As suggested above, the game could be played with cakes divided into halves, quarters and eighths. The dice can be altered accordingly, with two faces showing the values $1/2$, $1/4$ and $1/8$.

HOW TO PLAY PIECE OF CAKE

For 2 or 3 players

YOU NEED: cake cards (one whole cake divided into quarters and one whole cake divided into halves for each player), a fraction dice and a shaker.

❶ Each player chooses one of the cake colours.

❷ Decide whether you have to collect one or two whole cakes to win.

❸ Place all of the cake cards face up in the middle.

❹ Take turns to throw the fraction dice.

If you throw a fraction in your colour, you may take a matching cake card from the centre.

So: if you throw a ¼ in your colour, you may take a ¼ cake card from the middle. If you throw a ½, you may take a ½ cake card.

If you do not throw your chosen colour, you do not take a card.

❺ Continue playing. The first player to collect one whole cake (or two whole cakes) is the winner.

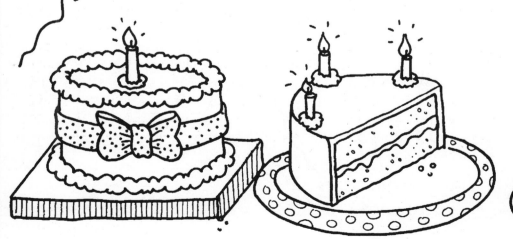

CAKE PIECES (1)

Colour the cakes on this page and page 117 using three different colours, so that there are two complete cakes in each colour (one divided into halves and one into quarters).

CAKE PIECES (2)
See instructions on page 116.

WHAT YOU NEED

PHOTOCOPIABLE SHEETS

Bingo cards sheet 121, multiplication spinner and checking card sheet 120, 1 to 10 number cards sheet 33, 'How to play' sheet 119.

FOR CONSTRUCTION

Card, adhesive (optional), scissors, a pencil.

FOR PLAYING

A bingo card for each player, multiplication spinner, a bag of 1 to 10 number cards, counters (nine for each player), 'How to play' sheet, checking board.

MULTIPLICATION BINGO

TEACHING CONTENT

☆ Learning multiplication and division for the two, five and ten times tables (N: 3c; MD: B)

☆ Using a calculator to check mental arithmetic (N: 3e; MD: B, C)

PREPARATION

Assembling the game: Photocopy sheets 33, 120 and 121 directly on to card, or mount on card after copying. Cut up the sheets to make the twelve individual bingo cards, the spinner, the checking card and the 1 to 10 cards. Push a pencil through the centre of the spinner and place the 1 to 10 cards in a bag. Nine counters will be needed for each player.

Introducing the game: Many children will be familiar with the concept of bingo from competitions in national newspapers. In order to play this game, the children will need to have been introduced to the 2×, 5× and 10× tables.

HOW TO PLAY

This game can be played by small groups or the whole class. Each player needs a bingo card and nine counters. The teacher, or a child, acts as the bingo caller and numbers are selected using a multiplication spinner and a bag containing number cards 1 to 10. The caller draws a card from the bag, then spins the multiplication spinner and announces the two numbers. The players then multiply the two numbers together; if the total is on their card, they can cover it with a counter. The children can work out the answer as a group activity if this helps. The card is then returned to the bag and play continues. The first player to cover all of the numbers on her bingo card is the winner. It is important that the caller keeps a record of the numbers that have been made, in order to check that the 'winner' has not made any mistakes. This can be done using the checking card, covering the numbers as they are called out. Rather than using counters, the players can cross off the numbers on their bingo cards as they are called; but a new card will then be required each time.

TEACHER'S ROLE

Once a number card has been drawn, ask the children what the possible totals will be after the spinner has been spun: what will the number be if we multiply it by 2, 5 or 10? Are any of these totals on their bingo cards? Once the two numbers have been multiplied together, look at the resulting number. Are there any other ways that this number can be made? During the game it is important that the children work out the multiplication correctly, so some guidance may be needed here. The game will give a good indication of which areas are causing problems. Encourage the children to work out their answers, explain their methods and then check their calculations themselves. If the mental calculations are causing difficulties, a calculator could be provided to check the total, or the players could refer to a written version of the times tables.

HOW TO PLAY MULTIPLICATION BINGO

For a small group or the whole class

YOU NEED: a bingo card for each player, the multiplication spinner, a bag of 1 to 10 number cards, counters (nine for each player, 23 for the caller), the checking board.

❶ Give each player a bingo card and nine counters.

❷ The caller takes a number out of the bag, then spins the spinner. She then announces the two numbers.

❸ The players then multiply the numbers together. If the total is on their card, they can cover that number with a counter.

❹ The caller also puts a counter on that number on the checking board.

❺ The caller puts the number card back in the bag, and play continues.

❻ The first player to cover all her numbers calls out 'Bingo!' Her numbers are checked against the checking board. If they agree, that player is the winner.

☆ REMEMBER!

Some totals can be made in more than one way. For example:

$2 \times 10 = 20$
$4 \times 5 = 20$

But you can only cover that number once!

BINGO CHECKING CARD

2x 5x 10x	2	4	6	8	10
12	14	16	18	20	5
15	25	30	35	40	45
50	60	70	80	90	100

MULTIPLICATION SPINNER
Cut out the spinner and push a
pencil through the middle.

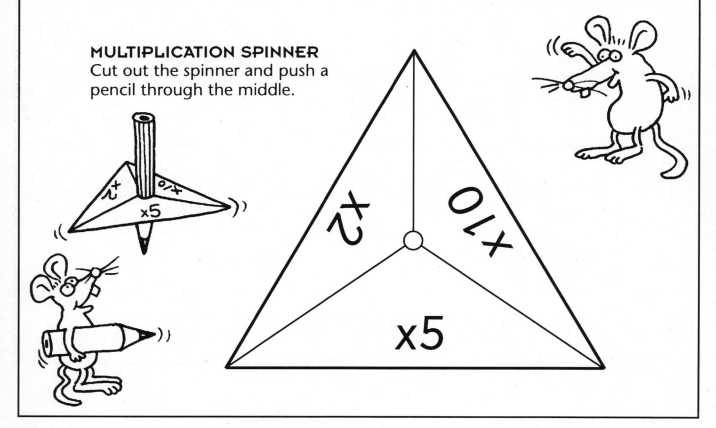

12	8	4	14	10	6	16	12	8
90	60	40	100	70	45	2	80	50
25	20	14	30	5	16	35	15	18
5	18	14	15	20	16	25	5	18
8	2	80	10	4	90	12	6	100
50	35	15	60	40	25	70	45	30
45	30	15	50	40	25	60	45	30
18	12	6	20	14	8	5	16	10
100	70	40	2	80	45	4	90	50
18	14	10	20	16	12	30	15	20
4	90	60	6	100	70	14	8	2
40	25	20	45	30	5	80	50	35

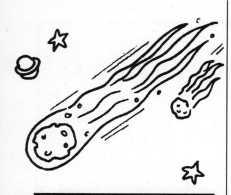

SPACE RANGERS

TEACHING CONTENT

☆ Use numbers in a flexible manner, seeing more than one alternative to numbers in play and positions on the board (N: 1a; FE: B)
☆ Experimenting with digits and number values (N: 1a; FE: B)
☆ Exploring multiplication and division patterns of 2, 5 and 10 (N: 3b; PS: B)

PREPARATION

Assembling the game: Photocopy the game board (page 125) on to thin card or paper. The board can be coloured in to make it more attractive. A coloured counter is needed for each player (red, blue, green, yellow). Two dice are also needed on which the 6 has been replaced with a 0 (cover the 6 face with a sticky label and write in the 0).

Introducing the game: This game can be given a story context to stimulate the children's interest. Perhaps the space station is about to explode and the spaceships are racing to rescue the inhabitants, or the spaceships are being chased and need to get to the space station for safety.

HOW TO PLAY

This is a game for two to four players. Each player takes a coloured counter (red, blue, green or yellow) and places it on the corresponding corner square of the game board. The players take turns to throw the two dice and make a number from the two numbers thrown. So: if you throw a 1 and a 4, you can make either 14 or 41. Players can only move their counter to an adjoining square if the number they have made is divisible by the number on that square. They are not allowed to move on to one of the meteor squares. In this example, it would be best to choose 14 at the start, since the first number needed to move must be divisible by 2.

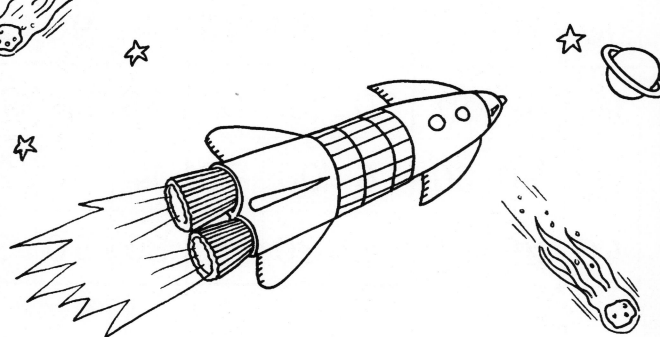

Play continues in this way. Players *must* move if they can make a number divisible by a number on an adjoining square – if they cannot make a number from the scores on the dice that is divisible by the number on one of the adjoining squares, then they cannot move (unless they throw 00, in which case they have another throw). The first player to reach one of the RESCUE (÷10) squares next to the space station is the winner. Play on to decide upon second, third and fourth places if you wish.

TEACHER'S ROLE

This game encourages children to use their 2×, 5× and 10× tables and, at the same time, requires mathematical thinking based on an understanding of how numbers work. Ask questions during play to make sure that everyone understands the game. What are the two numbers you can make? Can you divide these by any of the numbers on the adjoining squares? Do the other players agree? It is possible that a player will be forced to move backwards or even sideways across the board. If this happens, you can introduce the idea that if a player lands on a square already occupied by another player's counter, then the other player is sent back to the beginning. Look at all the possible throws for the 2× table, then go on to look at the 5× and 10× tables. What numbers appear in all three tables? What number endings appear in none of the tables? Use the 1 to 100 number cards (page 69) with the children for further work on investigating which numbers appear in which tables.

GAME VARIATIONS

A building block or dice can be modified to show the numbers 5, 6, 7, 8, 9 and 0 by covering the faces with sticky labels and writing in the new values. Again, look at which numbers appear in the 2×, 5× and 10× tables. What number endings do not appear in the tables? Are these endings odd or even? Are there any odd number endings in the tables? What number do they show? The board can be amended to include the 3× and 4× table for children of higher ability.

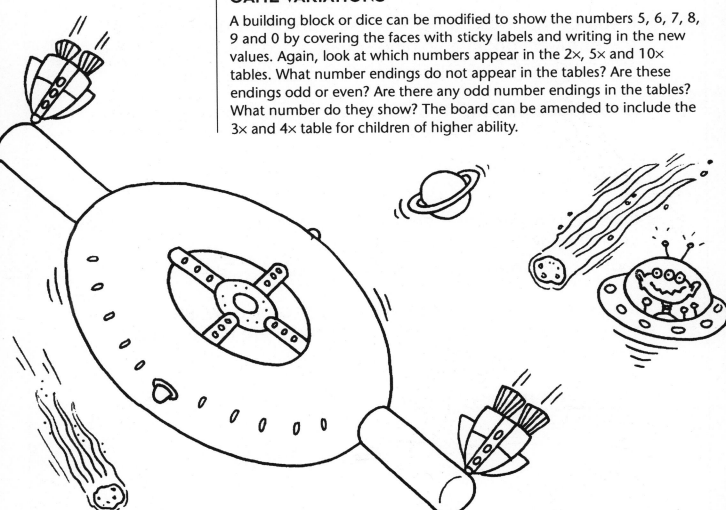

HOW TO PLAY SPACE RANGERS

For 2 to 4 players

YOU NEED: the game board, a coloured counter for each player (red, blue, green, yellow), two dice and a shaker.

❶ Place the counters on their matching 'start' squares (the blue counter on the blue square, and so on).

❷ Take it in turns to throw the two dice and use the two scores to make another number.

So: if you throw a 1 and a 4, you could make 14 or 41.

If the number you make can be divided by a number on an adjoining square, you must move your counter on to that square.

If you cannot make a number that can be divided by one of the numbers on an adjoining square, then you cannot move and must wait for your next turn.

❸ Continue playing. The first player to reach one of the RESCUE (÷10) squares is the winner.

☆ REMEMBER!

If you can make a number that can be divided by a number on an adjoining square, you MUST move – even if it means moving backwards or sideways!

If a player lands on a square already occupied by another counter, then the player who is already there is sent back to the beginning.

You cannot move your counter on to any of the meteor squares.

GREEN

YELLOW

÷5   ÷5

÷2   ÷2

÷10   ÷5   ÷5   ÷10

÷2   ÷2

RESCUE
÷10

Space Station
DOCKING   DOCKING

RESCUE
÷10

RESCUE

RESCUE

÷2   ÷2

÷10   ÷5   ÷5   ÷10

÷2   ÷2

RED   ÷5   ÷5   BLUE

STOP AND SHOP

TEACHING CONTENT

☆ Developing flexible methods of working with number, orally and mentally (N: 1a; AS: A)
☆ Counting collections and checking totals, using money (N: 2a; M: B)
☆ Using addition and subtraction facts to 100, using coins (N: 3c, 4a; AS: B)
☆ Using calculators as a tool (N: 1d; RTN: A)
☆ Recording and interpreting data (N: 5b; IH: A)

PREPARATION

Assembling the game: Mount the full-colour pull-out game board on to thick card and cover it with clear plastic adhesive to prolong its life.

This game is designed to be adapted to the specific number range the teacher wants to practise or reinforce. This could range from very simple bonds (to 10) all the way through to realistic decimal prices. Thus the number values are not printed on the game: they are decided on by the teacher and written on a copy of the group record sheet (photocopiable sheet 129).

A restricted 1 to 3 dice is needed. Cover faces 4, 5 and 6 of a dice with sticky labels and mark them with 1, 2 or 3 dots on faces opposite their corresponding numbers.

Introducing the game: Look at the game board with the children and explain that it represents a grocery shop. Identify with them all the items that can be bought. Ask questions such as: Do you go grocery shopping? Where do you shop? Do you go on your own or with someone else? How often do you shop? Show the children the group record sheet on which you have written the price for each item. Which one item would each child most like to buy?

HOW TO PLAY

This is a game for two to four players. The group record sheet (photocopiable sheet 129) is an integral part of the game.

Each player chooses a coloured counter and puts it on the appropriate coloured square of the board. Using a matching crayon or pencil, each player then writes in her name and colours in the appropriate shopping basket at the bottom of the record sheet. In turn, each player throws the dice, moves the number of spaces shown, then stops and shops (buys the item for that square). Items bought are recorded on the game sheet

WHAT YOU NEED

PHOTOCOPIABLE SHEETS
'How to play' sheet 128, record sheet 129.

FOR CONSTRUCTION
Full-colour pull-out game board, thick A3-sized card, adhesive, scissors, clear plastic adhesive, sticky labels.

FOR PLAYING
Full-colour pull-out game board, 'How to play' sheet, record sheet, up to four coloured counters (red, green, blue, yellow), up to four crayons or coloured pencils (the same colours as the counters), a restricted 1 to 3 dice, a calculator, coins (optional).

by colouring in one of the squares next to that item with the player's particular colour: R = red, B = blue, G = green, Y = yellow. Each player travels around the board in a clockwise direction, back to her own coloured starting square. In order to finish, the exact number required to land on this square has to be rolled. When everyone is home, the players total the cost of their own shopping (using a calculator to check or calculate as required), and the winner is the player with the highest total. The calculator can be ignored if the teacher wants to reinforce mental addition, or the record sheet can be used as a bill.

TEACHER'S ROLE

Ensure that the children understand the rules of the game and how the record sheet works. Intervene during play only if necessary. Afterwards, help the children to add up their bills and to check their answers with a calculator before filling in the total spent on the record sheet.

Ask the group: What is the most expensive item in the shop? What is the cheapest? What is the difference between the prices of these items? How did they arrive at this answer? Ask the children to add two items mentally; for example, what would the eggs and tea cost?

Depending on the number range chosen by the teacher, give each child a set amount of spending money (for example, 20p, 50p or £1). Ask, for example: If I had 50p and I bought the milk and soap, how much change would I receive? If children are having difficulty, provide them with some coins and allow them to work it out using the coins.

For more able children, move towards mental multiplication. For example, how much would two tins of beans cost?

GAME VARIATIONS

• Introduce an added element by making the coloured corner squares either penalty (lose a turn) or reward (move on one space) spaces.
• This game can be linked to 'Penny purse' (page 86) and/or 'Pound purse' (page 91), with children being given a purse full of money to spend in the shop. Be sure to have prices on the game record sheet that reflect the purse insert used. The winner could be the person who spent least rather than most money.
• Children could be given a set amount to spend and the person who spends nearest the total without going over is the winner. Instead of having to buy an item when they land on a space, they could choose whether to buy it or not. This involves a bit of forward planning, as well as some risk-taking!
• Bulk buy multiples of items instead of just one. Throw the dice a second time to determine the number of items bought. The price is then entered on the game sheet. The prices can be added up (as for a bill) by mental calculation or with a calculator.

EXTENSION

★ Recognising and using decimal notation in recording money (N: 2c; RTN: C)
★ Using multiplication and division to solve problems involving money (N: 4b; MD: C)

Adapt the record sheet to use decimal notation by deleting the 'p' symbols and inserting decimal prices.

HOW TO PLAY STOP AND SHOP

For 2 to 4 players

YOU NEED: the colour game board, a counter and crayon in each of the colours blue, red, yellow and green, a dice and shaker, a record sheet and a calculator.

❶ Each player chooses a matching counter and coloured crayon, and places her counter on the corner square of the board in that colour (the blue counter on the blue square, and so on).

❷ Fill in the players' names and colour in the shopping baskets on the record sheet.

❸ Now take turns to throw the dice. Move your counter that number of spaces around the track in a clockwise direction.

❹ Each time you stop, you must buy the item on that square. Use your crayon to colour in one of the squares in the left-hand column of the record sheet next to that item, to show that you have bought it.

R = red, B = blue, G = green, Y = yellow.

❺ Continue playing until everyone has been round the track and back to their starting square.

❻ When everyone has finished, look at the items you have bought and add up their prices. The player with the highest total is the winner.

☆ REMEMBER!

More than one player can buy the same item.

You must throw the exact number required to land on your starting square. If the number you throw is too big, that throw does not move you forwards.

RECORD SHEET FOR STOP AND SHOP

R	B			R	B		
G	Y	tea	p	G	Y	butter	p
R	B			R	B		
G	Y	jam	p	G	Y	ice-cream	p
R	B			R	B		
G	Y	beans	p	G	Y	burgers	p
R	B			R	B		
G	Y	cake	p	G	Y	soap	p
R	B			R	B		
G	Y	bread	p	G	Y	tissues	p
R	B			R	B		
G	Y	biscuits	p	G	Y	potatoes	p
R	B			R	B		
G	Y	milk	p	G	Y	carrots	p
R	B			R	B		
G	Y	eggs	p	G	Y	apples	p

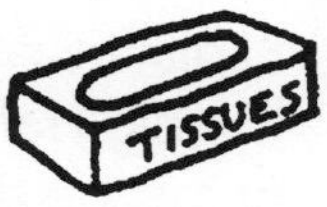

red

Name _____

I spent _____ p

blue

Name _____

I spent _____ p

green

Name _____

I spent _____ p

yellow

Name _____

I spent _____ p

STORYWOOD STARS

TEACHING CONTENT

☆ Developing flexible mental methods of working with number
(N: 1a; AS: B)

☆ Using addition and subtraction facts to 12 (N: 3c; AS: B)

☆ Recognising situations to which addition and subtraction apply and
using them to solve problems (N: 4a; FE: B)

PREPARATION

Assembling the game: Mount the full-colour pull-out game board on thick
card and cover it with clear plastic adhesive to prolong its life.

Introducing the game: Ensure that the children are familiar with the fairy
tales and characters represented on the gameboard, all of which have a
woodland theme: Goldilocks and the Three Bears, Snow White and the
Seven Dwarfs, Rumpelstiltskin, Hansel and Gretel, Little Red Riding Hood.
Explain that all the people who live in Storywood are story stars and, like
the big Hollywood film stars, they don't like to be ignored. So during the
game, on their journey through the wood, each player must visit them all!

HOW TO PLAY

This is a game for two or more players. Each player, in turn, throws the
two dice and decides whether to add the two resulting numbers or to
subtract the smaller from the larger. So: if a 2 and a 4 are thrown, the
player can make 6 (which is 4 + 2) or 2 (which is 4 – 2). He then moves
his counter the number of spaces indicated by the answer. Each player
must visit each character and, in order to do this, must make the exact
number required to move on to the character space each time. If he
cannot make the exact score required, that throw does not score. More
than one player can occupy a space at any one time. The first player to
reach FINISH, with an exact number, is the winner.

TEACHER'S ROLE

The teacher should distinguish between children who are just performing
the easiest arithmetical function and children who are moving towards
employing a game strategy to determine which function is more
appropriate for reaching the next character space. Are the children

anticipating what number they need to reach the next character space, and calculating what numbers they might need to throw next? Ask the children: With a small gap such as the one between the Miller's Daughter and the Three Bears, do you think addition or subtraction will be the best method? Why? What about a big gap such as the one between the Three Bears and the Big Bad Wolf?

GAME VARIATIONS

To make the journey through the wood slightly more difficult, introduce a 'question card' element. Make up a set of at least 40 cards with number sentence problems or story problems (perhaps related to the fairy-tale characters), or a mixture of the two, on them. For example: If you go to visit the seven dwarfs but three of them are out at work, how many are left? When children land on a character space, they must take a card from the pile and answer the question correctly before moving on. The card is then replaced at the bottom of the pile. If they answer incorrectly, they must wait until their next turn before taking another card. If that question is answered correctly, they can move again on their next turn.

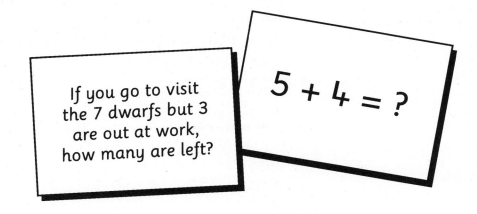

FOLLOW-UP

There are many opportunities here to extend the fairy tale theme into language work. For example, children could work in pairs, one being one of the story characters, the other being an interviewer. What questions would the interviewer like to ask? What would the characters say about themselves?

HOW TO PLAY STORYWOOD STARS

For 2 or more players

YOU NEED: the full-colour game board, a counter for each player, 2 dice and a shaker.

The aim of the game is to reach the end of the track, but on the way you must meet ALL of the Storywood Stars. This means that you have to land on all of the squares with a character on them.

❶ Take it in turns to throw both dice. The two numbers will be used to make your score.

❷ Each turn you must decide whether you want to add the two numbers together or subtract the smaller number from the larger.

So if you throw a 4 and a 2, you can add the numbers:
$4 + 2 = 6$

or subtract them:
$4 - 2 = 2$

❸ Choose the score that is best for you and move your counter that number of spaces.

❹ The first player to land on the finish is the winner. Again, you must throw the exact number to win.

☆ REMEMBER!

You cannot pass a Storywood Star square without landing on it. If your score is too many, that turn does not allow you to move forward.

More than one player can occupy one space at the same time.

MATHS
KEY STAGE
ONE
1
GAMES

Special section

ABOUT THIS SECTION

The resources in this section comprise components for three board game contexts, with boards based on a 4 × 1 layout. In addition to being used for a number of games with specific mathematical objectives in this book (i.e. 'Fire! Fire'! – page 47, 'Hop it!' – page 51, 'To buy a fat pig' – page 56 and 'To market, to market' – page 60), they can also be used for games with other mathematical and/or cross-curricular objectives.

The 4 × 1 layout uses four identical photocopiable sheets to create a large game board for four players, each with his own playing track. Each game has a 3-D centrepiece with varying functions: sometimes a focal point or decoration to stimulate interest and imagination, sometimes a goal to aim at. In 'Fire! Fire!' the burning house is a passive object in terms of the game, but it excites interest with its flames and adds urgency to the proceedings; the water lily is the finishing point in 'Hop it!'; the fenced marketplace in 'To buy a fat pig' and 'To market, to market' is both a receptacle for the animals and a place of business.

In addition to forming the basis for the game board, the individual playing track can also be used in a number of other ways:

• It can be a record sheet. For example, an individual child can chart his own individual progress, marking the exact spots landed on. Or it can be used as a group record sheet, with each child using a different coloured marker.

• It can be a small game board in its own right. With just a little adaptation to track and game rules, it can become the game board for a pair of children, or even a single player competing against himself.

• It can be taken home to share with family members or to play individually. Counters or coins can be used for playing pieces; a small bowl or something similar can serve as a finishing point or receptacle.

CONSTRUCTION OF THE 4 X 1 GAME BOARDS

All the game boards in this section are constructed in the same way. The playing track is copied four times and any surplus paper outside the border trimmed away. Colouring the boards will add enormously to their appeal. Instructions for any specific colour detail for individual games are given below. Otherwise, be as creative as you like!

The sheets are then mounted on to card 445mm × 445mm and the centrepiece is put or glued in place. (For construction of the individual centrepieces, see the photocopiable pages.) Laminating the finished board is optional, but will increase its durability and prolong its life.

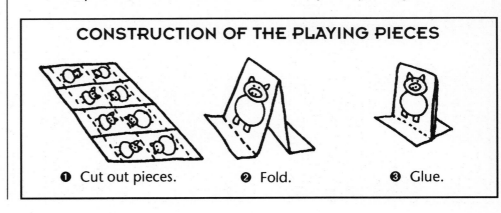

CONSTRUCTION OF THE PLAYING PIECES

❶ Cut out pieces.   ❷ Fold.   ❸ Glue.

FIRE! FIRE!

- Playing track (page 139)
- Centrepiece (house) and fire engine playing pieces (page 140)

Colour each fire engine a different colour (red, green, blue or yellow). Then colour each of the fire stations and their adjoining 'start' squares on the tracks in matching colours.

HOP IT!

- Playing track (page 141)
- Centre pieces (water lily and base) and frog playing pieces (page 142)

Colour the frogs red, blue, yellow and green as indicated, then colour each of the 'start' stones on the tracks in matching colours.

TO BUY A FAT PIG AND TO MARKET, TO MARKET

- Playing track (page 143)
- Centre piece (market fence) and Land Rover playing pieces (page 144)

Colour the Land Rovers red, blue, yellow and green as indicated, then colour each of the farms on the board in matching colours.

CONSTRUCTION OF THE GAME BOARD

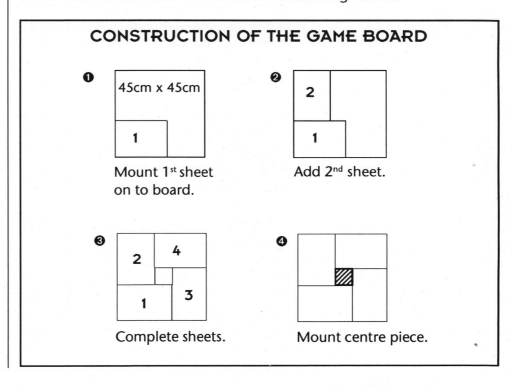

❶ 45cm x 45cm — 1. Mount 1st sheet on to board.

❷ 2, 1. Add 2nd sheet.

❸ 2, 4, 1, 3. Complete sheets.

❹ Mount centre piece.

FIRE! FIRE!

HOP IT!

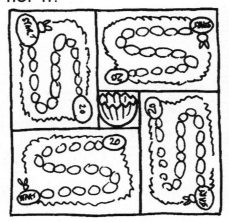

TO BUY A FAT PIG AND TO MARKET, TO MARKET

FURTHER IDEAS FOR CLASSROOM AND HOME USE

The photocopiable games, of which these 'Special section' resources are a part, are very much enabling games. That is, they provide a context into which mathematical objectives are injected. This means they can be applied to other maths or cross-curricular objectives, or be used to add a fun dimension to a particular theme. For example, the 'Fire! Fire!' playing track could be adapted to have basic shapes rather than numbers in the squares, to make identification of shapes an objective. 'Hop it!' might be used as the basis for science work on animals and their habitats. 'To buy a fat pig' and 'To market, to market' fit easily into the topic of farms and farming.

Each of the three contexts represented by these resources provides many and diverse opportunities for language development. Storylines could be developed and extended. For example, 'Fire! Fire!' can be the basis for a strong sequential narrative with all the drama of the discovery of a fire. Whose house was on fire? What caused it? What were the flames like? Was there much smoke? What did the people in the house do? How did the fire engine sound as it sped through the streets? How did the firemen put the fire out? All the time, the teacher will be drawing on examples from real life: Have any children had a fire at home, or seen fire engines at a fire (even if only on television)? A word list of topic-specific vocabulary can be written on the chalkboard. The 999 emergency procedure could be discussed. The themes of the other games could be developed in a similar vein. What they all offer to children is simulation of an experience which can serve as a bridge between the imagination and the physical task of communicating thoughts. The game board provides a surface upon which not only to play but to extend skills of invention.

FIRE! FIRE!

Emergency 999

Add a sense of urgency and a focus on time measurement by making the time taken to get to the fire the winning factor. Each player plays all the way to the end before the next player's turn, timing how long it takes. If a timer is not available, the number of dice throws could stand for time. Keep a tally of how many throws are taken to finish a game (including 'penalty' throws). An individual could play this a few times and try to beat his own record. An exact throw must be made to get to 30.

Hazard!

Emergency vehicles can often be delayed by road hazards. Use the game to practise recognition of multiples by choosing a table, say the 5× table. Any player landing on a multiple of 5 encounters a hazard and misses the next go. Discuss with the children what sort of road hazards might be encountered.

Fast track

Practise mental subtraction. Two dice are needed. Throw the first dice and move the number of spaces indicated. Leave the first dice where it is. Then throw the second dice. If the number on the second dice is more than the number on the first dice, the player calculates the difference and moves that number of additional spaces. If the second dice throw is the same or less, no further move is made on that turn.

In sequence

Players can only move in a sequence of 1, 2, 3, 4 and 5. If they throw a 6, they can have another go. This means they have to keep thinking about the last throw. (But if they forget, how can they work it out? *By starting at 1, then adding 2, then adding 3 and so on.*) When they reach 5 in the sequence, they go back to 1. To finish, a 5 must be thrown.

Put out the fire

In this variation, players must not only reach 30 with an exact throw, but (to win) must then put out the fire by throwing a 6 (or any other pre-agreed number).

HOP IT!

Short hops

Use a 1 to 6 dice, but players can only move forward on a 1, 2 or 3 throw. If 4, 5 or 6 is thrown, the player must hop back one space (if he is on the Start square, the player does not move). If a player lands on a black stone, he must go back to the Start. An exact throw is needed to finish.

Catch a fly

This is a game for two players. Place 'flies' (counters) on each of the black stones. If a player lands on a black stone, she can take a 'fly' (counter). The player with the most flies at the end wins. Players can choose to move forward or back on the throw of their dice, so children need to be aware of the effect of both forward and backward moves.

Snapper pike

This game for two players is the reverse of the above. In this game, the counters on the black stones are pikes which like to eat frogs. If a player lands on a black stone, she must take the counter. The player with the fewest counters at the end wins. If a player accumulates three counters, she is deemed to be a dead frog and her opponent automatically wins!

Hopalong

For this game, which practises recognition of odd and even numbers, players take no notice of the black stones. They play the game twice. The first time, players can only move when an even number is thrown. An exact throw is needed to finish. What is their record speed for reaching the end? They now play the game moving with odd numbers only, and compare records. Which was the faster game, the even or the odd? (Note to parents/teachers: Add up the even numbers on the dice faces and add up the odd numbers. Compare the two, and you will see which has the better chance.)

Two hops forward, one hop back

In turn, each player throws two dice and adds up the scores. Then he throws a single dice and takes this away from the double dice number to find the number of spaces forward he can move. If the single dice number is bigger than the double dice total, the player stays where he is. Players must go past 20 to finish.

TO BUY A FAT PIG

Market day

Instead of allowing only one pig to be bought per visit to the market, players can buy one each time they land on a market parking space. As well as seeing who has the most pigs at the end, see which player has bought the most pigs in any one visit. If a child is playing on his own, he can play several times and try to increase his single-visit buy each time.

Pay up

For this variation, each player is given an agreed number of £1 coins (say ten). When he lands on a market parking space, he has to throw the dice to find out how much the pig costs. For example, if he throws a 4, he must pay four £1 coins. If he doesn't have enough money, he must wait until his next turn and try again. Which player gets the most for his money in the end?

Sell a pig

This variation is the reverse of 'Pay up' above. Depending on the number of players, they all have a set number of pigs to *sell* at the market. When they get to the market, they throw the dice to see how much they will

get for their pig. They then collect their money and leave the pig at the market. The player with the most money at the end wins.

Sell fast

Make the game a race against the clock to sell the pigs. Each player starts with a set number of pigs. Set the timer. The first player throws the dice. This gives the number of pigs he can put in the Land Rover. He puts the pigs in, and continues to throw the dice to take them to market and return to his farm. He keeps doing this until he has taken all his pigs to market. An exact throw is needed for the last pig or pigs. So if a player has four pigs in the farmyard and throws a 5, this will not do. He has to throw again until he throws a 4 or less. How long did it take? Can the next player do it more quickly? If a timer is not available, count the total number of throws.

20 throws

Each player is given 20 throws of the dice. How many pigs can he buy in 20 throws? If a turn ends before a player gets back to his farm, the pigs in the Landrover can still count towards a win. Encourage the children to keep track of the throws on a piece of paper. This would be a good opportunity to introduce them to tallying.

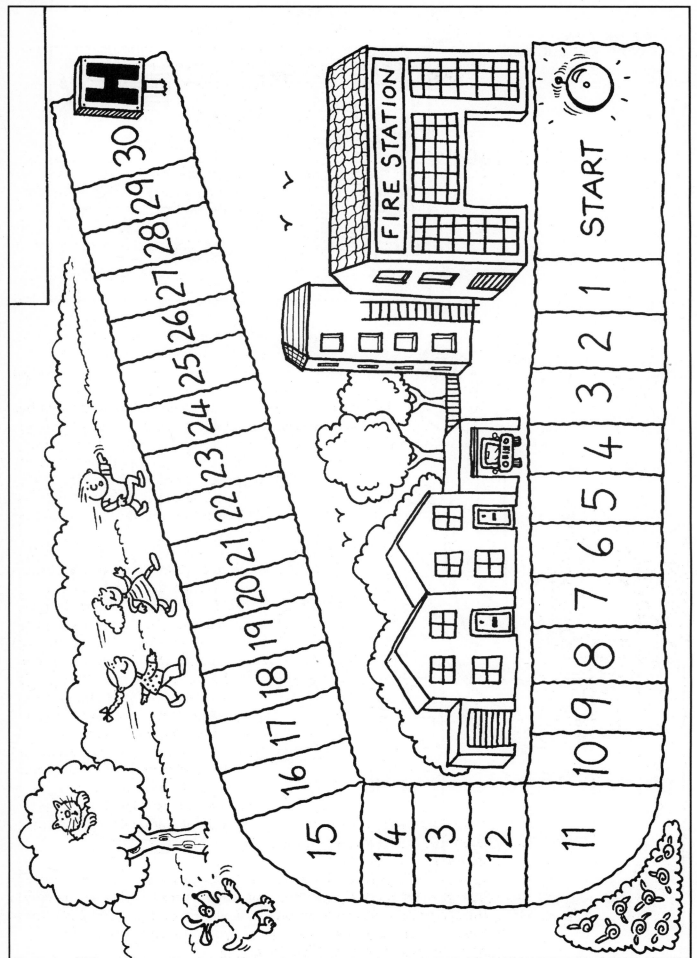

❶ **PLAYING PIECES**
Colour, cut out, fold, glue and hold.

❷ **CENTRE PIECE**
Colour, cut out and fold each piece then glue them together.

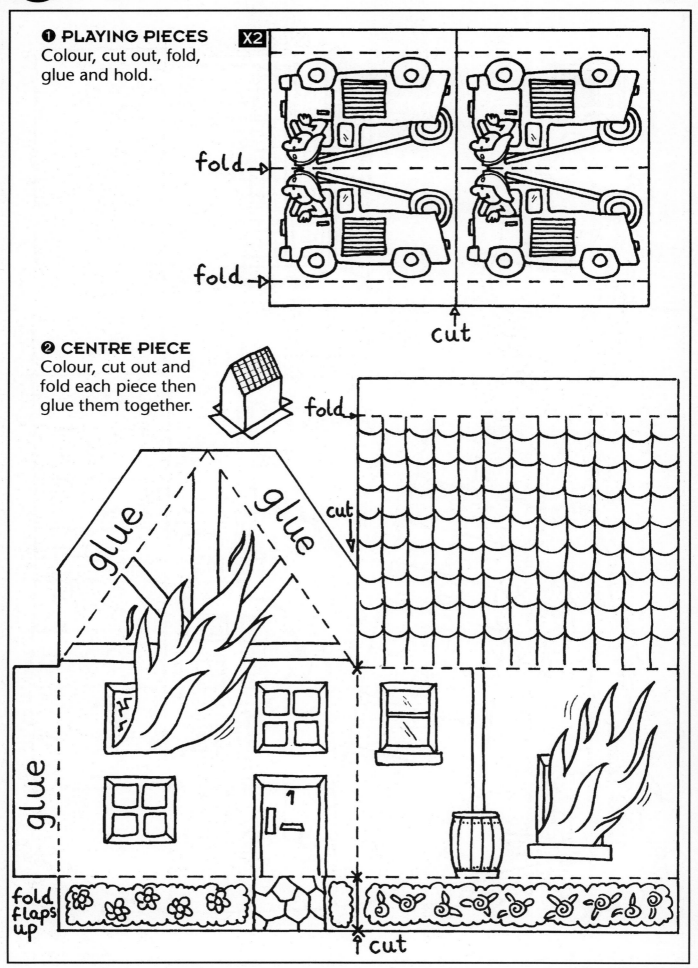

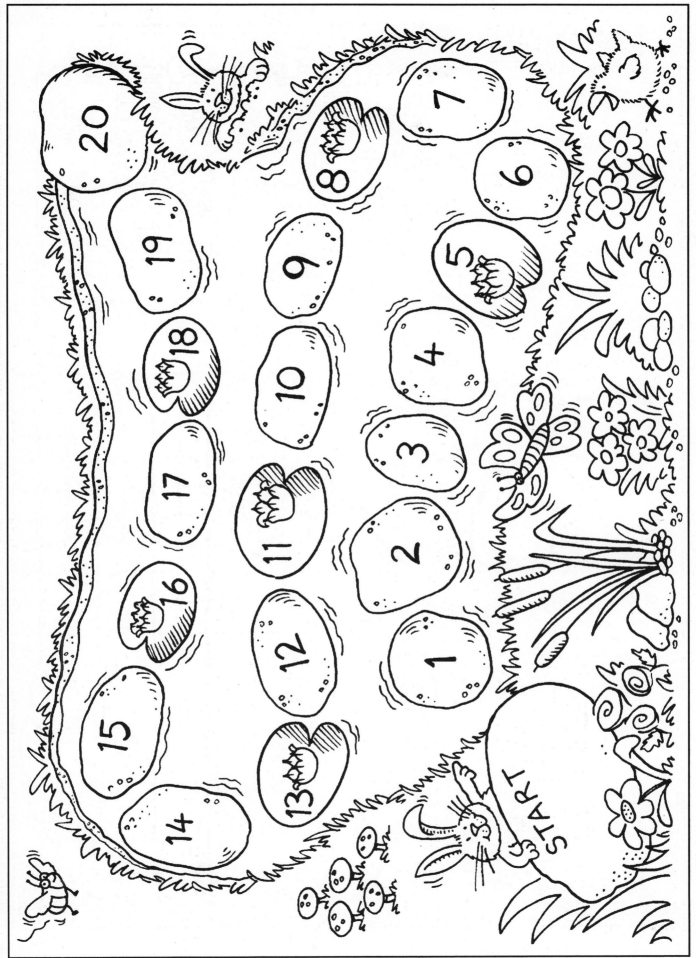

❶ **PLAYING PIECES** X2

Colour, cut out, fold, glue and hold.

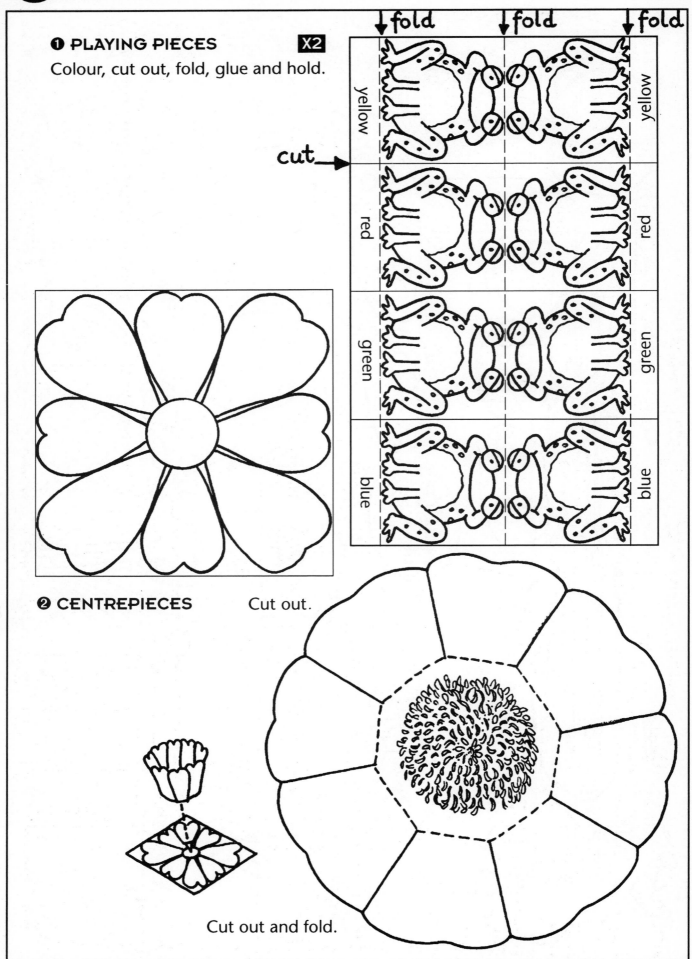

cut →

fold   fold   fold

yellow   yellow

red   red

green   green

blue   blue

❷ **CENTREPIECES**   Cut out.

Cut out and fold.

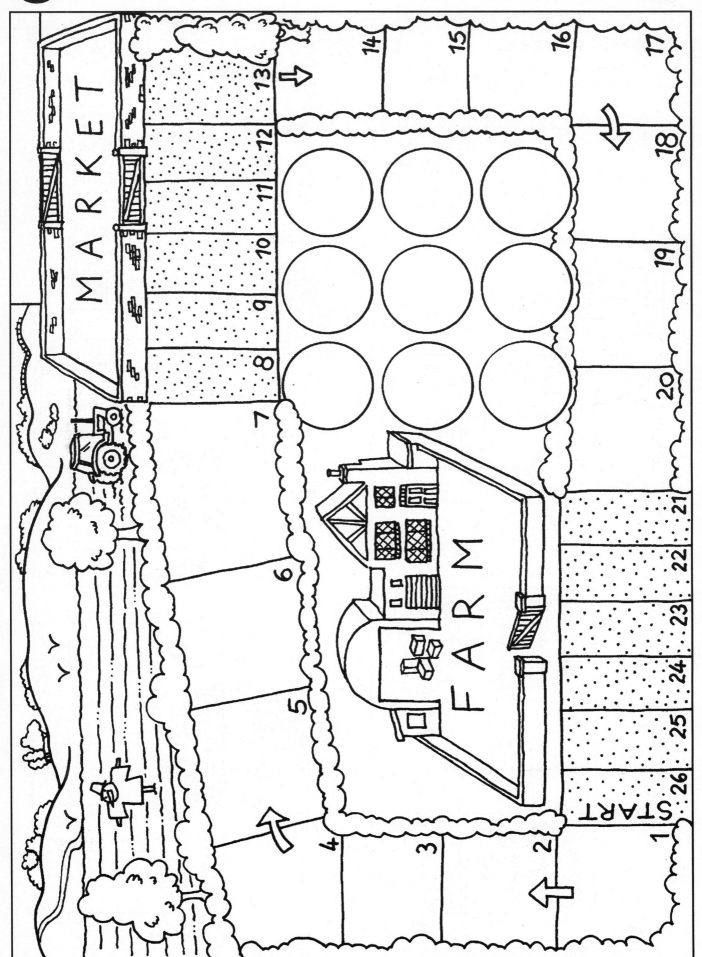

x2

❶ PLAYING PIECES

Colour, cut out, fold, glue and hold.

❷ CENTRE PIECE

Colour, cut out, fold,
glue and hold.

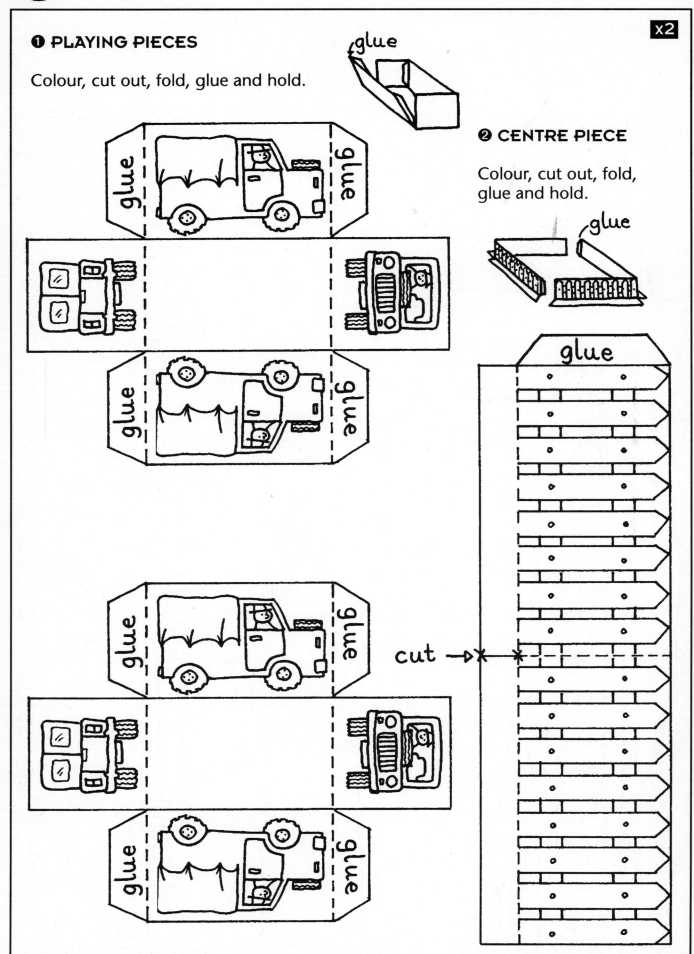